Travel, Research and Teaching in
GUATEMALA AND MEXICO
In Quest of the Pre-Columbian Heritage

Travel, Research and Teaching in
Guatemala and Mexico
In Quest of the Pre-Columbian Heritage

Volume I. Guatemala

—◆—

Mark Curran

Professor Emeritus
Arizona State University

Order this book online at www.trafford.com
or email orders@trafford.com

Most Trafford titles are also available at major online book retailers.

Printed in the United States of America.

ISBN: 978-1-4669-9249-8 (sc)
ISBN: 978-1-4669-9248-1 (e)

Trafford rev. 04/29/2013

 www.trafford.com

North America & international
toll-free: 1 888 232 4444 (USA & Canada)
phone: 250 383 6864 ♦ fax: 812 355 4082

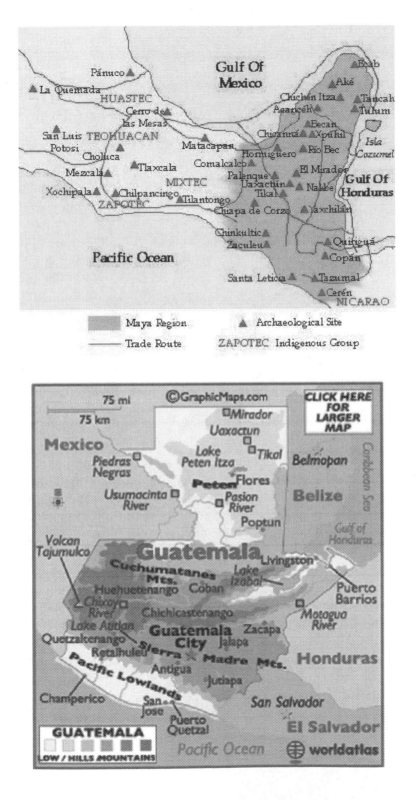

Volume III in the Series: Stories I Told My Students

Table of Contents

II. FRANCISCO MARROQUÍN SUMMER SCHOOL IN 1977

LIST OF IMAGES

PREFACE

My love affair with Mexico, Guatemala and the Pre-Colombian cultures of both nations began long before I really had any awareness of the latter. As told in "Coming of Age with the Jesuits," my first reason for travel to both countries was to have a practical experience in Spanish after "book learning" from two years of study of the language in Abilene High School and three years of classroom study at Rockhurst College in Kansas City, Missouri.

That first foray to Spanish America in 1962 was an adventure in itself. I studied for approximately three months in the summer school of the "Universidad Autónoma de México" in Mexico City. The small town farm boy from Abilene would live in the gigantic metropolis and be exposed to just a taste of the grandeur of Mexico City. But following the study in Mexico I would experience the absolute beauty of southern Mexico and Guatemala when I took the bus, a 35 hour ride, to the Guatemalan border, via Puebla, Oaxaca, and Tuxtla Gutiérrez, where I boarded a "school bus" on to Quetzaltenango, Guatemala, and a rendezvous with college buddy Eduardo Matheu. This good friend to this day introduced me to the wonders and beauty of that country, especially to Lake Atitlán and Chichicastenango, and then to Antigua and the Pacific Coast, and to the hospitality of his family. There were adventures, a lot of Spanish was learned, but most of all, the experience convinced me to continue study in Spanish and Latin American Studies on the graduate level and make it part of a lifelong endeavor. Earning a Ph.D. in Spanish and Latin American Studies at Saint Louis University in 1968 would open the door to this new world.

After beginning a teaching career at Arizona State University in 1968, I returned to Guatemala for a short visit in 1969 after a research trip to Brazil. Eduardo met me at the airport, took me to the family home and then to a "churrascaria" in the downtown to cure my homesickness for Brazil ("matar saudades"). We then did a short trip, Eduardo, his charming friend Fabiola, and I, to the Duchez and Matheu family farm at Vista Bella where Eduardo was dealing with the planting of fruit trees. The trip included a look at the flour mill, "Molino Venecia" which neighbors Vista Bella, and then a trek on horseback to the Iximché Ruins of the Mayas. Then we motored to Lake Atitlán, via Katok for dinner, then to Sololá, Panajachel, and hiked a trail to the Matheu cabin. Eventually there was a canoe ("cayuco") ride across the lake back to Panajachel, our drive to Chichicastenango to see its famous market and church and back to Guatemala City.

In 1969 Keah and I married with only a quick honeymoon in Arkansas (she was from Little Rock where the marriage took place). The real honeymoon took place the following summer when I had a research grant to Brazil for study of its folk-popular poetry. After time in Recife,

Salvador and especially Rio de Janeiro, the summer was almost at its end. But I had promised Keah we would have a quick stop in my first love, Guatemala. So at the end of August, 1970, I introduced Keah to that country. Memories are a bit hazy now as I write this, but for whatever reason, we ended up on a tour, a whirlwind introduction to the country. We traveled by VW Van to Antigua, Lake Atitlán and Chichicastenango, and Keah and I stayed at the "Casa Contenta" on the Lake. Suffice to say, Guatemala had not lost its charm.

These three encounters, 1962, 1969, and 1970, were the cornerstone for the edifice that would be built later. But it was in 1976 and once again in 1977 that serious study and research of not only the land and the history, but mainly the Maya would come into play. And even then there is an added note. One of the minors for the Ph.D. was indeed Latin American Studies. I always was attracted to history, economics, and geography and such, perhaps more than to literature and literary criticism, even though the latter was the main thrust of the Ph.D. at Saint Louis. So when I casually asked to teach the course "Spanish American Civilization" at ASU in about 1974, the former professor and colleague Roberto Acevedo willingly offered me the opportunity. I jumped at the chance. And in fact I "inherited" the course for the next 25 years. Teaching civilization meant one had to indeed be a "jack of all trades, master of none," and to have a broad knowledge of myriad aspects of all Latin America. The first step in any decent civilization course has to be the beginnings, that is, Pre-Colombian Latin America. So one finally arrives at the topic for this book—Travels in Guatemala and Mexico and the Pre-Colombian Heritage of Mesoamerica.

I say "Mesoamerica" because even though I had traveled to Peru in 1967, I was not attracted to the dry, stony Andes, and had only the rudiments of knowledge of the Inca Civilization, even though it merited great attention. It was simply that the beauty of Guatemala remembered from 1962, the land, the forests, the rich volcanic soil that produced an incredible agriculture, and the colorful vestiges of an old civilization beckoned me, once again admitting that at this point I knew little about them. But the Spanish American Civilization course required that I would know much more. So I immersed myself in study of Mesoamerica and its Pre-Colombian culture, just to be prepared to offer a decent course.

As a result of a sabbatical in Colombia in 1975, in the recent book "A Trip to Colombia and Its Highlights of Spanish Colonial Culture" (Trafford. 2013) I expressed admiration for that beautiful Andean country. But in 1976 and 1977 fate would have it that in fact I would "change direction." Arizona State University had established a summer school in Guatemala City in 1974 at the Universidad Francisco Marroquín ("the Harvard of Central America"). The original director had moved on, and the job was offered to me. All this I mention as preamble because it really is in 1976 and in Guatemala that serious study, reflection and life-long enthusiasm for Meso-America really began.

Intensive travel and study would take place in Guatemala (and to a lesser extent Mexico) in 1976 and 1977. A long hiatus would follow—back to endeavors in Brazil—but the passion would be rekindled in an intensive trip to Mexico in 1998, then in less serious endeavors in Cancun in 2000 and Cozumel in 2002.

This book, third in the series: "Stories I Told My Students", will tell the tales of those years and I hope will express the enthusiasm, joy and rewards of the endeavor. At the end of the book are appendices which explain in greater detail some of topics of the book; these are more "academic" in tone, thus the decision to use the rubric of "appendices."

A disclaimer by the professor: there are several good reasons why I do not delve more in this narrative into what is seen and its possible meaning. The first is that I do not have the credentials to do so, i.e. archeologist or anthropologist specializing in Meso-America. What I do possess is a sense of curiosity and admiration for all that we have seen, but probably more directed to the visual captured in hundreds of photographs. Over the years I enthusiastically read anything I could get my hands on pertaining to the topic, i.e. classic books and especially any articles from National Geographic Magazine. But I found that the more I read the "less" I knew, always recalling the statement of a scholar whose name I do not recall, "With the Maya, all is always more than it seems." But as a result of all this reading I also discovered an important thing: the experts themselves to not agree on the meaning of things, and one constantly notices the words "perhaps, possibly" and the like in their own narratives when referring to concepts, buildings, images and decorative objects. No doubt the deciphering of most of the Maya glyphs in recent decades has aided immeasurably in knowing some things "for certain," but even then, the experts admit that "much is to be done." I liken the whole thing, a bit, to religion and the existence of God: it cannot be proved, but as Joseph Campbell said, "Where would that leave faith?" Thus it is the "mystery" of much of the Pre-Colombian that is what in fact fascinates me. So be it.

PART I. SUMMER SCHOOL IN GUATEMALA IN 1976

INTRODUCTION

Because I had spent a short bit of time in Guatemala in 1962 after a summer school session in Mexico City at the UNAM, because the professor who started ASU's Summer Program at the Universidad Francisco Marroquín in Guatemala City had left the program (perhaps because of tenure problems), and because of my general interest in Latin America, I was drafted to run the Summer School in 1976. I might add that at this time there was a lull in possibilities in Brazil, so I "changed direction" to Guatemala. I do not think there was anyone else at ASU free at the time, or with the inclination to "chaperone" students, or frankly a more "politically correct candidate." (How much more of a minority can you be than a white, Irish, farm boy from Kansas whose first language was English running such a program?) Such was the atmosphere in academia at the time. I did possess the main criteria: a genuine love and interest in returning to Guatemala and an ability to both recruit and get along well with the students.

I guess it is the eventual fate of all foreign language teachers to run a "program abroad" or at least participate in one. So this was my lick at the ice cream cone. It was a good opportunity for travel since our daughter Katie had not come along yet, and my wife Keah was amenable to go, so we agreed to do it. In the end it was a mixed experience. I had a strange mixture of talents and likes for the Department of Foreign Languages at ASU. I appreciated literature and culture, but yet was not so esoteric that it made an oddball of me. I have a degree in Business Management and am very practical and organized about certain things, yet management was not my cup of tea. I enjoyed being around GOOD students and liked to travel. The trouble is, as I soon learned, you do not necessarily get "good" students in such a program. Naïve to be sure, we plunged ahead.

An aside: I recall how the "drafting" for the job took place. The Director of the Latin American Center at ASU, Professor Lewis Tambs of the History Department and as I wrote these notes, ambassador of the United States to Costa Rica after a stormy tenure in Colombia, invited me to a decent lunch (not the campus variety) with a beer or two in a nice place near campus. He flattered me for a while and made the invitation. It all seemed a romantic adventure at the time. Oh, there is another factor (these are the stories I did not tell my students), after success at the summer research grant business in 1969, 1970, and 1972, summer teaching and camping on our newly acquired acre in Colorado in 1973 and 1974, I hit a streak of a couple of negative responses on national NEH grants, was down and feeling a bit unworthy of it all, so the Summer School (recall I had just spent a delightful sabbatical once more in Spanish America, in Colombia in 1975), seemed like a viable and fun alternative to the race of "grantsmanship." Strange are the motives that move men's minds.

I thoroughly enjoyed the recruiting process during the academic year prior to the summer session: making up the advertising brochure with some good Guatemalan art, working with Tom McCrea of the Tempe Daily News, and the visits to classes to "sell" the program. In all humility, yes, I was very good at that sort of thing. I dressed up in a Guatemala Indian jacket, brought some slides and talked it up. Most of the students as might be expected were from a large Spanish section at ASU with just a sprinkling of folks from off-campus—SMU, Vanderbilt and a couple of other kids. Some fun students I had the pleasure of teaching in Portuguese classes signed up too. I thoroughly enjoyed the public relations and the initial meetings. That all turned out to be the easy part! Professor Tambs did not say that; he said the "fun" would begin when we got on the plane.

An aside: from now on, the travel notes, the notes on cultural sites in Guatemala and Mexico, and most importantly much serious reading and study would be part of the annual course, SPA 472, Spanish American Civilization, each spring at ASU. So indeed the places we shall see and the tales I will tell will be an important part of that course. The serious part would begin in 1976.

THE FLIGHT TO GUATEMALA

After a restless night in anticipation of the trip, we flew Western Airlines to Los Angeles at 7:30 a.m. and then transferred to the big Western DC 1011 for the flight to Mexico City. We were exhausted before we even left. I thought at the time that it was convenient that we could check luggage all the way through to Guatemala, how pleasant! Keah and I were traveling with two of the students; most had arranged their own transportation, many by bus or train, and stories are to come about that. Mexico City airport was smoggy (an understatement) and unpleasant on the whole, although our five hour layover was not as bad as it could have been, with the people watching and all. But we were miserably tired.

Aviateca, the Guatemalan answer to the air age, was one half hour late; it turned out to be a pink colored plane, a DC 9 from Brazil's rummage sale I think (interior signs were all in Portuguese). But it was a very smooth flight of one and one half hours to Guatemala City and first class service, including a scotch and light dinner before landing at night in Guatemala City.

The city was beautiful from the air. Professor Rigoberto Juárez-Paz (Philosophy, University of Minnesota) and local director of the summer school program met us at the airport in his old, beat up, little car. Customs was not crowded and was in fact leisurely, and it was a new airport done in good taste. My small bag with all my clothing was missing, and after a bit of a run around at Aviateca, we left with promises that it would arrive the next flight down from Mexico. I recall the air smelled humid, but was pleasant with the scent of the fires the Indians still used in the shanty towns in the suburbs. It was rather warm, 75 to 80 degrees Fahrenheit.

"EL HOGAR DEL TURISTA"

Our home for the next five weeks would be the "Hogar del Turista," the Tourist's Home, a Latin "pensión" in Zona 1, Calle 11, 10-43. It was very near the downtown center, off 6a. Avenida, the main thoroughfare, and really not too far from the old main plaza with its Cathedral and National Palace. It is to be noted that a major earthquake hit Guatemala in February of that year; there were many deaths and massive damage throughout the land. There was some doubt we would indeed have the summer school, but we were assured in Tempe, Arizona, that everything was all right. But this part of the city was badly hit by the quake, and buildings all around were cracked or even destroyed. We would feel tremors and aftershocks more than once at the "Hogar."

The Indian Maids, "Hogar del Turista"

Professor Mark in Maya Finery, "el Hogar"

The owner was a German lady, María Mertins, a widow with more than forty years living in Guatemala; she owns two "pensiones" and a "granja" or farm outside of town. One of the benefits of the later is a constant flow of fresh roses and other flowers brought in daily to decorate the place. The "Hogar" is delightful in a quaint way: dark wood decoration, tile floors along the corridor, and a pleasant dining room. We got to know the Indian maids well—Mercedes in the dining room and old Anita from Quetzaltenango mopping up. There were dozens of plants along the main corridor, and songbirds in cages throughout. Our room was simple, but had a private bath and shower, twin beds, a tiny desk with ample light when opened to the corridor. It was decorated with Guatemalan Indian decorations with the blankets from the lake region, tapestries and table covers. All reflected the Maya heritage of Guatemala.

Food is well prepared and tasty: eggs, juice, coffee, and good "pan francés" for breakfast; soup, beef, potatoes, beets, good vegetables, meatloaf and fruit for other meals.

THE ADVENTURE BEGINS: ARRIVING AT UNIVERSIDAD FRANCISCO MARROQUÍN

Mark in Coat and Tie at UFM

The next day is Monday and it all begins. I really tried to fit in and fill the role, dressing in sport coat, tie and dress slacks each day in the accustomed Latino professional manner. Good ole' bus number 1 arrives from 6a. Avenida and we arrive in twenty-five minutes at the university which is in Zona 10, an upscale area of the city.

The main building is an old mansion, the administration building, with some modern buildings surrounding it, and with large shade trees.

U.S. Consul Harold Gross arrives for a little welcome talk, the last we heard from him or any other U.S. personnel; he was not the slightest bit friendly or hospitable to Keah or me. It chafed a bit. We met Vera Aguirre, the guiding light for the entire summer, the main secretary involved with the summer school who organized student housing and handled hassles. She was terrific, wonderful and more!

Organizing classes was a bit chaotic, but it finally got done. Professor Juárez-Paz did the entire scheduling on the blackboard. In retrospect, that was probably a good way to do it. Some students signed for the Antigua trip the next day, the first planned outing. The excursions for the summer were a continual headache and hassle; this one was obligatory, and there was much moaning and groaning on the part of some of the students. So the next morning twenty weary travelers showed up, including Connie and Terri, former students in my Portuguese classes at ASU who had taken the bus from Tempe to Guatemala! No small accomplishment! Students had many stories of rip-offs from taxis, etc. in Mexico, and particularly at the border with Guatemala. Had things changed so much since 1962 and my own similar adventures?

After that first day at school we returned to the pension for the "almuerzo" and a siesta. After an attempt at a nap, unsuccessful, we then walked up to 6a Avenida and its shops and then down to the big plaza to the Cathedral. Inside the huge edifice one is a bit nervous; the central nave is all right except for the cupola which is entirely cracked. The side corridors are totally closed up and the ceiling is completely cracked. We were constantly assured that all had been inspected and we were safe.

Guards at the National Palace

Maya Sacrifice, the National Palace

Conquistador Alvarado Battles the Mayas

Then we moved on to the National Government Palace, "el Palacio Nacional." It was impressive with murals of Don Quixote and Sancho Panza, others of Pre-Colombian Mayan scenes, and best of all the "sala de recepción," the Reception hall, with its fantastic glass chandelier, gold-gilt ceiling, images of Quetzales, the Guatemalan national bird and name of its currency, and beautiful rosewood furniture.

A sobering post-earthquake note: in the park in front of the palace there were poor people living in plastic covered lean-tos.

Then it was home to the "pensión" to read the paper and quaff one or two Gallo Beers. It was rest for the weary. But during the night we felt small quakes, aftershocks I guess. We don't like to talk about it.

There is no baggage yet, thus no clothing for Mark. Keah is a real trooper and is learning some Spanish. Tomorrow is the first outing, to Antigua.

FIRST TRIP TO ANTIGUA

An Overview

The city of Antigua was founded in the 16th century, following the original capital in Iximché in the highlands after the final conquest of the Indians by the Conquistador Alvarado, one of Cortez's lieutenants in the Conquest of Mexico. After Iximché the capital was moved to Almolonga, a few kilometers outside of Antigua proper today, but that site was damaged seriously by the "Volcán del Água" with serious flooding and later on by earthquake. Subsequent to that time, activity was centered on the site of Antigua itself. One should note that massive earthquakes would continue to play a role and plague Guatemala; Antigua was ravaged once again by quakes in the 18th century when the capital was definitely moved to Guatemala City where it thrives today.

So Antigua in effect became a small jewel in the history of the country due to the vestiges of its location, its beauty, its proximity to major Indigenous centers with their rich culture, and its own monumental architecture. The Plaza de Armas with the Palace of the Captains' General, the 16th century convents of the Capuchins and Claritians (religious orders originating in Spain but more recently moving down from Mexico), the original San Carlos de Borromeo University and the outstanding colonial churches of the Merced and San Francisco are only some of the major reasons for the importance of the city.

One needs to recall the role of Guatemala as one of the "Capitanías Generales" of colonial Spanish America set up by the Crown of the Hapsburgs in Castile; these geographic, administrative and population centers were second in importance only to the larger Vice Royalties that surrounded them. And one needs to recall that for a few years after Independence from Spain, it was the Kingdom of Guatemala in the early days which included the State of Chiapas in Mexico and some of the neighboring countries like Belize, El Salvador, Honduras and Nicaragua of today's modern Central America.

The Trip

After breakfast at the "Hogar," and the bus on 6a. Avenida to the university, Professor Juárez-Paz took me to the airport where after a horrible hassle we retrieved my lost luggage. Then, joining the students, it was on to Antigua via a Kombi (VW Bus) of Guatemala Sightseeing. We passed through the outskirts of Guatemala City and the industrial zone, then began a gradual climb to pretty green hills that overlook the city.

Washing Clothes at an Indian "Pila"

There was a short stop at the town of San Lucas where there is an Indian "pila" or fountain and well, where many natives were doing wash, all dressed in colorful Mayan clothing. The town and its church seemed to have been mostly destroyed by the quake just a few months earlier in 1976, but we were all amazed by the smiles and friendliness of the natives.

We then arrived at the intersection for the Antigua cutoff, and a local market was set up at that point. Buses must take the long way around passing through Chimaltenango since the short road to Antigua was covered in many places with "derrumbes" or slides resulting from the quake (shades of our travels in Colombia just one year earlier). There was ample evidence of the devastation of the earthquake.

After Colombia in 1975 and contrasting Antigua to it, the general aspect of the place in 1967 seemed at first a bit depressing to me; it seemed very poor, much was in ruins, and in fact the whole town seemed to be one large ruin. Keep in mind, the people at Universidad Francisco Marroquín assured us in the spring of 1976 that "everything was all right in Guatemala." Its saving grace indeed that summer would be the people, the Indians and their friendliness. This observation was shared by some of the students, discerning in nature, who would conclude during the summer that in fact the country was a mess, in ruins, but what wonderful people!

On the way to Antigua we were shown a coffee plantation with small trees now flowering. Large shade trees are needed to shade the coffee plants. Thus there are jacaranda trees for shade planted many, many years before coffee production. It is easy to imagine the investment—not only of money but of time, for the entire process can take from eight to ten years. One needs to hang on, and I imagine, and to have deep pockets.

Keah and Local Weavings, San Antonio Aguas Calientes

After the coffee plantation we were taken to see the "barracas" or tourist stands of San Antonio Aguas Calientes outside of Antigua where we looked at truly magnificent weavings, some of the nicest in my view of all Guatemala. The kids from ASU were impressed. One could see the devastation of the town itself by the 1976 earthquake, particularly the church which was in effect destroyed.

The Old Church at Almolonga

Guatemalan Sightseeing then took us to the old part of Antigua where the kids clambered around the ruins. This was the "original" capital of Guatemala in the 16th century after the conquest and Iximché and was known as Almolonga. Some of the remaining buildings are still impressive in spite of the original damage from quakes in the 16th century when the Spaniards decided to move the capital to the present day site of Antigua. We saw the original cathedral in what is called "Ciudad Vieja."

Mother, Daughter, Vendors, Main Plaza, Antigua

Children Selling Dolls, Boy with Ice Cream Cone, Main Plaza, Antigua

From there we were taken to Antigua's central plaza where there was marimba music, Indians selling wares, and the kids loved it. We all had a great lunch, picnic style in the plaza, the students sharing sandwiches with Indian children, bargaining for purses, belts, etc. There was time in the interim to see the central plaza, the old Capitanías building, the cathedral, and the Universidad de San Carlos Borromeo.

Sightseeing continued after lunch, first to the Recolección Ruins and then to the magnificent church of La Merced. The Convent of the Capuchins came next. Its damage reflected the first major earthquake in 1773, and many have come since, the most recent now in 1976.

View of Antigua and the Volcán del Água

Equestrian Statue of Pedro de Alvarado, Conqueror of Guatemala

The trip ended with a drive to the top of the "cerro" or hill overlooking Antigua which has as its focal point the huge statue of the Conquistador Alvarado and to a "required" stop at a weaving shop with looms (to stimulate business for Guatemala Sightseeing). This was followed by the impressive San Francisco Church. We noticed the famous Star of David below one of the altars but were told that it did not necessarily refer to any Jewish connection. There was a large altar to the side with dozens of photos for "paying promises," that is, either thanking the saints for wishes fulfilled or praying for needs to come, There were golden lions painted in the dome. A more factual description of what we saw that long day is as follows.

Architecture in Antigua

The architecture in Antigua is of the 16th century; it is a combination of Spanish Renaissance, Italian and Moorish. In effect the town is a jewel of Spanish colonial architecture.

From the Moors one sees patios or inner courtyards with fountains and flowers. Also Moorish are the simple outer walls, ornamental only on the windows and doors. This is opposed to the stucco facades and ornamentation of Italy.

The upper arcaded corridor used as a sightseeing gallery and promenade is a prominent feature of the Captain's General Palace in Antigua. Such galleries were features of Renaissance Spain and incorporated in the major cities of the Viceroyalties, i.e. Mexico, Peru, and Colombia.

The influence of Spain is seen in the chiseled stone porticos and paneled or studded doors on many buildings as well as turned wooden grills on windows and stone fountains.

The 16th century simplicity seen in so much of Antigua was later replaced by the baroque flamboyance of 17th century, seen mainly in some of the churches.

Points of Interest in Antigua

All the above can be seen in these points of interest in Antigua:

The "Portal" or doorway of the "Convento de Nuestra Señora de la Concepción" at the entrance to Antigua. It dates from 1694. There is a stucco frieze depicting "La Virgen de la Concepción." One sees the sun above and the moon below her feet, the Spanish coat of arms to one side, the knight-saint Santiago to the other. The convent itself was founded in 1578 by four nuns from Mexico. It included Doña Juana de Maldonado, the "favorite" nun of Antigua's first Bishop, Francisco Marroquín!

La Plaza de Armas

It was originally known as the "Plaza Real." It was reserved for jousting and bull fights. There were as well indigenous festivals which portrayed scenes from the Conquest. The Plaza also served as a market place. The fountain was to one side, the gallows on the other!

El Palacio de las Capitanías Generales

The Palace of the "Capitanía General de Guatemala"

The Palace dates from 1764, nine years before the massive, destructive earthquake. It was the residence of the man with the lofty title of "Gobernador, Capitán General y Presidente de la Real Audiencia." Guatemala had been included in the broad plan of the Spaniards after the conquest. The main centers of Spanish dominion in the Indies were of course the Viceroyalties, four of them: Nueva España (Mexico), Peru, Nueva Granada and Río de la Plata. Smaller areas bordering the viceroyalties but administered separately became the Captaincy Generals, among them Cuba, Guatemala and Chile.

El Palacio del Ayuntamiento. The Palace of the Mayor and Town Council

La Catedral.

It once was considered the most beautiful building of the capital. It was begun by the same Bishop Marroquín in 1543 and not finished until 1680. Guatemala's most famous conquistador and conqueror of the country, Pedro de Alvarado and his wife Beatriz de la Cueva were buried in the building, but since the earthquake the tombs are not seen.

The statue of "La Imagen de la Virgen del Socorro," originally from Spain and from the original church in Almolonga in 1538, is now in the Cathedral of Guatemala City. One recalls, once again, that "old" Antigua, to coin a term because it all is "old," was called Almolonga. The original town site was almost totally destroyed by an earthquake in the 16th century, and the capital was moved to present day Antigua.

The University of San Carlos Borromeo.

Interior Patio of the Museum of San Carlos Borromeo

Painting of San Ignacio Loyola, Founder of the Jesuits

The funds for its construction came from Bishop Marroquín. It was finished in 1678 and at that time was the largest university in Central America. Its architecture is principally Moorish as can be seen in the arches of the corridor around the central patio. The stone, chiseled doorway was added in 1843. Legend has it that the university was known for the belief of its students in the "True Faith."

The Street of Santa Catarina.

The Arch and Walkway over Santa Clara Convent

There are several prominent features, among them, the arch itself over the street. The arch which at one time was empty or vacant supposedly became a corridor by which the nuns passed from one side of the street to the other. Tattling tongues insist it was for "liaisons" between the nuns and local priests. The convent itself dates from 1609.

Mark and Keah the Santa Catarina Convent

The House of the Lions

Stone Portico, la Posada de Don Rodrigo

Marimba Band, the Patio of the Hotel

"La Casa de los Leones" with its carved portal and windows is a very impressive sight on the same street. The interior patio of the building, an upscale lodging place in 1976, was replete with beautiful gardens, parrots and an Indigenous marimba band playing for the tourists.

La Iglesia de la Merced (The Church of Mercy)

The Façade of La Iglesia de la Merced

It was built by the Mercedarians, one of the first religious orders to arrive in Guatemala. Some of the main features are the stone fountain in its atrium and the statue of Fray Bartolomé de las Casas. Fray Bartolomé arrived at Almolonga in 1536 and dedicated himself to learning the Quiché language and making translations from the same to Castilian. It would be he who would bring the final peace to the Departments of the Verapaces in northeast Guatemala. And of course, later on he would be known as the champion of the cause of all the Indigenous peoples, telling the story in the famous "Breve Descripción de Destrucción de Indias" ("The Brief Description of the Destruction of the Indies"). An irony of the matter is that Las Casas himself was purportedly a plantation owner in the Dominican Republic which employed Indigenous labor.

La Iglesia de San Francisco

Façade of the Church of San Francisco

The Red Robed Jesus

The Blue Robed "Virgen Pastora"

This was the original site founded by the famous Fray Motolinía from Mexico in 1544. The church is known for its façade decorated with the "twisted" columns and 18 carved statues of saints. It was seriously damaged by the earthquake of 1917 (and one might add the recent one of 1976).

BACK HOME TO GUATEMALA CITY AND THE "HOGAR DEL TURISMO"

On the way home from Antigua the highway was very crowded, people returning from a weekend in the country. The city was hazy from above. We returned to the "Hogar" for beers, a cigar for the professor and a supper of chicken.

Local Characters in the Pensión. There was Bruno from Germany, a tool and machine salesman, and travelers from all of South America, and one from as far as Angola in Africa. Good conversations were held with Manolo and Hector Ricardo from Buenos Aires. And best of all there was a visiting classical violinist from Honduras about to present a concert in Guatemala City.

Some students now are ill with cough; Mercedes, the younger Mayan maid, gave one student medicine she says is made out of extract from skunk oil!

There were five tremors while we were gone, the strongest at 3.8. But you could feel them for sure.

Keah says we are getting along great with the students at the pensión. And the food is good. Keah is doing well in the intermediate Spanish class and complementary of Mark's spirit and good teaching in the civilization course. Do I note any bias in these last remarks?

The canaries in the cage at the boarding house are covered each night with a cloth by the maid Anita. It keeps them quiet most of the time.

FIRST ACTUAL DAY OF CLASSES

All went well I thought considering we did not have any textbooks. They would arrive only much later and this caused some consternation both on the part of the students and the professor.

After that first day at UFM, we spent the p.m. wandering about the downtown: shops, to Guatemala Sightseeing, to friend Eduardo Matheu's old office where he worked with his brother Julio selling veterinary products, to the central plaza, to "la Regional," a neat crafts shop, and to Tuncho's bookstore.

Keah is speaking more Spanish; great for her, a real adventure. A perfect compañera!

Time goes by. Classes are okay. There is a problem with one of the girls: we get the word she is too bossy at her home, giving everyone orders. And she won't take a bath. The Guatemalan family wants her moved.

Another day: there is a pleasant surprise. Upon leaving class, there is Eduardo! Now with a big black beard! And Kit his Californian wife. They took us to a Spanish restaurant, Altuna, Calle 12, with excellent "paella" (shrimp, jumbo shrimp, white chicken and pork on a bed of rice).

Eduardo and Kit had returned to Guatemala in 1971. He had done graduate work on horticulture at the University of California, Davis, where he met Kit. Previously he had done two years of undergraduate work at California State Polytechnic College for his degree in fruit production. Upon Eduardo's return to Guatemala he first sold veterinary products and then worked for a flower exporting company. His aunt, Sor Elena Duchez, a Sister of Charity, who was in Panamá, sold him her part of the farm Vista Bella in the Guatemalan highlands, so they are now on the old farm I first saw in 1962 where he has plantings of alfalfa which he dehydrates and sells to horse owners in addition to the apple orchard he started.

Eduardo told me that when he came back from studying "hands on" fruit production and after doing graduate work that he prided himself on not being a gentleman farmer (most coffee farmers in Guatemala are gentleman farmers). He was very happy about the fact that he was working in the fields and teaching the workers how to manage the orchards and grow vegetables.

He told that before the huge earthquake in 1976, by chance, two days earlier, he had ordered the heavy tile to be taken off the roof, replacement for leaks, etc., and this probably had saved their lives—there was no heavy tile roof to fall in on them. The other wing of the house fell in and also the machinery shed. The farm's chapel was destroyed. They invited us to the farm after classes are over.

We had time to attend movies in Guatemala City and saw "Three Days of the Condor." $1.50 quetzales was the price of admission, but one could pay 50 cents for the wooden seats in the "peanut gallery." And there were wooden benches in the back.

Heavy rain at times stopped us from going to the bus stop. Just "hurry up and wait" is the order of the day. Indeed, the rainy season had arrived in Guatemala. Many times we were set to do something and a downpour interrupted the plans. The best thing to do then is stay in for a siesta! With the metal roof on the pension, it was great sleeping. But the students moan and groan.

Classes. They are proceeding all right in my opinion: today was the first use of slides and the "go" for the final class lists. My funny office (I had requested office space as a criterion of accepting the job) was a cubicle on the newly added second floor in back of the classrooms. No one else was up there. I looked at it once and never went back.

Buses some days are extremely crowded, undependable, real "cucarachas" and we are even late to class some days.

Keah says there are 20 students enrolled; some mal contents, but most okay. But responsibility is weighing on her as well!

Keah writes of her contentment just to be there; it is a big adventuire.

Lunch at the pension that day was beef, guacamole, tortillas, watermelon and café. With the downpour it was just fun to sit at the desk with the window open, looking at the orchids and flowers in the patio and just listen to the rain. After it stopped, we went for a pleasant walk downtown.

The days continue at UFM. Bus # 2 is old and rickety and a mess, but quicker than walking to 6th Avenue and waiting. Mark is now on tea with a stomach disorder. With all the rain, my classroom is a quagmire; one has to be careful with the electric cord for the slide projector. I am short of material for SPA 201 and hope to use the local paper "La Prensa." There is moaning and groaning by the students about the lack of text books. I had to call A.S.U. to see where the books are.

At the same time the kids are now adjusting to life in Guatemala. There are lots of new "relationships," some of the girls hitting it off well, maybe too well, with wealthy Guatemaltecos. And some still have housing problems. C'est la vie! Today there was a downpour when getting off the bus at 6a. Avenida, and it continued on the walk down the hill home. But we enjoyed taking a nap under warm Indian blankets and dozing with the rain. I am reading up on Tikal. Some of us went to town at 6 p.m. for a Cantinflas film, "El Ministro y Yo." I understood everything except some slang terms; it gave me great nostalgia for old Mexico City days.

Musing on Downtown Guatemala City

Downtown is interesting, but not anywhere as impressive as Bogotá or Rio or not to mention Mexico City. This should be no surprise as Guatemala City is small and has the atmosphere of a small city-capital. There is a poor aspect to it as well, a dark atmosphere; I attribute most of this to the horrendous earthquake. I guess one must realize that this is really a small country and very poor at that and not to expect the grandeur of a more prosperous place. This has not prevented a huge difference in social class arising—the contrast between rich and poor. Keah and I, so far, are not seeing the comfortable side of things as I did in the past with the Matheu family. It produces a little different perspective. What saves the total experience are the trips to the very beautiful countryside.

The Next Day and the Work Week

It was a good day at school: bureaucratic stuff in the a.m. including a letter to the Summer School Dean at ASU, Mr. Kigin, with the report of class lists, credit-audit list, pass-fail list, passport numbers, books, etc.

The Reception on the Lawn at the UFM Campus

The University certainly went out of its way to welcome us all in a semi-formal reception on the lawn near the administration building. We did feel a bit more a part of things after this social moment.

Profesor Juárez-Paz, Kcah, Vera and Others at the Reception for ASU at
Universidad Francisco Marroquín

Marimba Band at the Reception.

There was a keg of beer, all kinds of "entremeses" (snacks) of "comida típica guatemalteca,"
not really so different from the same in Mexico. They provided a marimba band which was terrific
and the students had a good time. I would have a lifelong love of Guatemalan marimba music

and still have old 33 rpm disks of the same. I must say it was a very nice effort at welcoming us all to Guatemala and to the UFM; well done! Everyone seems primed for the trip to Tikal and the ruins tomorrow. After the reception we went with students Connie, Ann Clelland and John Cassidy to Restaurante Altuna for "paella." This was followed by a great conversation with the students at the pensión.

A MAJOR MOMENT IN FUTURE STUDIES AND INTERESTS: THE FIRST TRIP TO TIKAL

An Introduction to Tikal

This major Mayan archeological site is a jewel of the Classic Period from approximately 300 to 900 A.D. It is located in thick tropical rain forest in the Department of the Petén in northern Guatemala and is close to several other important sites like Yaxchilán and Uaxactún. The site is sometimes used in an analogy as the "New York" of the Mayas referring to the immense height of several of its pyramid-temples (as opposed to the "Paris" of the Mayas at Copán in Honduras for the complexity and art of its carved stelae). It is also located in a national park and much of the pleasure of the site is found in experiencing the forest, the animals such as howler monkeys, immense flocks of parrots, and even the cutter ants we saw at work in the forest. The site is large, some six square miles. It was discovered in 1848, rediscovered in 1877 and again in 1904.

The area was populated as early as 600 B.C., but Tikal came into its own between the 6th and 9th centuries A.D. Once thought of as a city of "peaceful philosophers" by early students of the Maya, it is now known because of the successful deciphering of the hundreds of Mayan glyphs that the dynasty of kings of Tikal ruled in despotic fashion and was in fierce competition for territorial expansion with neighboring city-states such as Calakmul and later on Quiriguá. There is now confirmed evidence of war, bloodshed, capture of enemy soldiers and to some extent human sacrifice, thus contradicting the really "romantic views" of the early scholars.

But notwithstanding the above, Maya accomplishments in tropical agriculture, conservation of water, the art of sculpting its historic markers, the stelae, and the painting of ceramics with the same "glyph markers," and perhaps most importantly, the monumental construction of its temples are indeed to be reckoned with. The Mayan language in effect made it possible for them to write history in stone and ceramics. And the interest in astronomy and the long-count in Mathematics allowed them to achieve knowledge and greatness. The pantheon of Mayan spirits and gods is a story in itself. The important historic link between the leaders of early Tikal and the magnificent civilization of Teotihuacán in central Mexico marks an important part of their history and early development.

The Site Itself

It is both a park and archeological site and no population is allowed in it. The many monuments include:

Pyramids 1,2,3,4,5
Stelae representing kings, nobles, and warriors; these are monolithic sculpted stones of 2 to 3 meters in height with images on one or two sides and with glyphs on the others explaining the stone which is really a historical marker.
The North Acropolis: smaller temples with some tombs
The Central Acropolis: smaller temples with some tombs.
Twin Pyramid Complexes built each "Katun" or twenty years

Diary of the Trip

Guatemalan Sightseeing picked us up at the "pensión" and we traveled to the old Guatemala City Airport (the one I knew as the new one back in 1962 when Eduardo Matheu and I flew to Mexico City, spent my 21st birthday in a big blowout at the Tenampa Bar, famous for its mariachis, and then went by bus from Mexico City to Kansas City and home to Abilene.)

DC-3 Airplane at Guatemala City Airport

The plane in 1976 to Tikal was an Aviateca Twin Engine Convair. All seemed well organized; the airline agent had all the tickets which I distributed to our group. Until takeoff we spent time watching planes depart for Puerto Barrios on the Atlantic. There were many old DC-3s from the Guatemalan Air Force about, but also DC-4s, Convairs, C-47s and small jets. (The large jets are of course at the modern terminal on the other side of the airport, that is, the international flights.)

We took off on time in the clouds and rainy weather heading to Tikal. It was a smooth flight, no problems at all. One does note that this route occasionally suffers a disaster because of extremes in tropical weather; just a few months ago there was one. There was a good aerial view of Guatemala City after takeoff and we enjoyed a light breakfast aboard. At one point we descended below the clouds and were low enough to get a very good idea of the rain forest in Guatemala; it was dense like I remember the Amazon. We then passed Lake Petén with its blue-green water.

The "Plaza Mayor" of Tikal from the Airplane

And then, suddenly, there appeared the pyramid temples of Tikal! It was truly an amazing moment; they were all very near, all in sight and I got great photos partially because we flew once around the field (to scare off people and dogs?), landing on a very, very narrow landing strip surrounded by trees and forest. We were in the midst of the tropics. The view of the several pyramids of Tikal from the air at that moment is still one of the most outstanding memories of then and now adventures in Latin America.

Everyone had to reconfirm their place on our return flight to Guatemala City in the tiny shack that served Aviateca on the strip, and then we climbed aboard a blue school bus and were off to the "Hotel Posada de la Selva" or "The Jungle Inn." Little did we know then, but we were experiencing a bit of tourist "history." I was given to understand later that the government had closed the "Jungle Inn," probably for a lack of hygiene or perhaps for "guerrillero" activity in the area. In later years all tourists must land at the airport in Flores (capital of the Petén) and take buses for about an hour's drive to the site.

In our days lodging at the site consisted in the "Posada de la Selva" or "Jungle Lodge" with thatch roofs, some little "casitas" to the side, and with two "long houses." Flowers and birds were everywhere and one hears a lot of noise from the forest. I'll have more on the actual Inn a bit later after our exploration of the ruins.

Arrival at Complex Q

Professor Mark at Complex Q, "Yada yada yada."

Complex Q. Maya Arch, Stela and Altar

The archeological zone is divided into various "complexes," nine in all. Each consists in two small pyramids with several stelae in front which serve as monuments and historical markers.

There was intense heat, especially with that hot, tropical, jungle sun. They bused us first to Complex Q which consisted in a small pyramid with nine stelae in front, but the latter were not carved. Nearby there was a small building where you could see small round altars and sculpted stelae under a Mayan arch (the small building had no roof since the originals were of thatch, long gone with the ravages of weather and time). It was believed these complexes were built each "katun" or twenty years. These, yes, came up to my expectations from photos and books perused in the U.S. prior to visiting the site. The figures on the stelae in Complex Q were not very clear, but one needs to recall the site was developed only 1300 years ago!

We moved on to Complex R, an unexcavated site where the stelae were now covered with tree roots, rocks and soil. There is a pyramid like in Complex Q but it is totally covered by a hill. We are told this is because there is a lack of money for the excavation. I recalled that in 1962 when I visited Teotihuacán outside of Mexico City that the famous Pyramid of the Moon was only partially excavated. These things take time and money. Over the years since Guatemala and the UFM experience, I assiduously followed articles in "National Geographic" and their documentaries on television which described recent new discoveries and excavations. I'll tell of these as the narration passes, but suffice to say there were wonderful new discoveries and the world came to know and understand much more of the Mayas.

Still on the main road to the central plaza, we passed by a tunnel dug into the back of the Acropolis. Its purpose was to study the different phases and levels of construction of the Mayans through the decades (and centuries) on the Acropolis. And of course they discovered tombs beneath this large complex.

Arrival at the "Plaza Mayor" or Main Plaza

"Templo del Jaguar Gigante" or Temple I

The first view of this impressive place is amongst the highlights of all Pre-Colombian Mayan sites. It was really something! When one walks through the narrow corridor to the side of Temple II into the immensity of the Plaza one is literally overwhelmed with the grandeur of it all—Temple I at one end, Temple II at the other, and the Acropolis del Norte to one side and the Acropolis Central to the other. And the sides of the Acropoli and fronts of the temples are lined with the most impressive carved stelae of the site. All in all it is a huge courtyard. In its totality it was not the slightest bit disappointing from previous pictures, but bigger than life, mysterious, of another world, in sum, exotic!

The students were converted into monkeys, scrambling up the temples in a flash. I was not so quick to make the climb but stood watching, impressed by the grandeur of it all, first of all for the size, but then by the total aesthetic effect of the entire complex, the temples and the closed plaza, a metropolis from the past!

Mask of "Tlaloc," Influence of Teotihuacán

To the side of the plaza is the Central Acropolis where there is a large Tlaloc—Rain God, one of the enigmas of the site. Tlaloc was not a "native" Mayan god, but rather from Teotihuácan in central Mexico. As time went by, this entire story was revealed by the scientists—the fact that in the very early days of Tikal there was indeed a Teotihuacan priest-chieftain who would be instrumental in the formation of what would be one of the grandest sites of the Mayas! In 1976 one climbed down into an opening in the side of the Acropolis to see the image which has the traits of Teotihuacán and was covered then by a simple sheet of corrugated tin to keep off the rain. One recalls the large ear plugs of the image.

Keah, Stela and Glyphs

Back up above we inspected the row of stelae and I dutifully documented them all in slides. Some of them I had recognized from books and National Geo magazines, but at this point they were the best I had seen at a real archeological site. The stelae were representations of nobles-priests-warriors with scepters, jade ear rings, nose plugs, breast plates and such, all highly ornately carved in the stones. Suffice to say, the Mayan stelae of Tikal are of stone, one stone at that, perhaps six to seven feet tall. There is generally one carved figure on one side (the stones are four sided), but perhaps with another on the opposite side. On the lateral sides there is often a Mayan text, carved in stone. On the belts and breastplates of many are depicted images of Mayan spirits and gods. These texts then have on one or two sides the famous glyphs of the Maya language. In 1976 only a few were deciphered, but since then almost all the Maya glyphs are known due to work by the great Linda Schele and David Stuart and other "Mayanists." There is an immense literature dealing with all this, from the early book by Morley, to the latest by David Stuart and colleagues. What Morley thought earlier on were simply glyphs telling of numbers and dates, we now know that in effect they were telling the "story" of the figures depicted on them, in effect, historical markers. It was Linda Schele who emphasized that Maya "History" begins with these stone monuments, a carved history to be sure. One discovers that the Mayan language as seen in its glyphs would evolve, grow and one day be forgotten, and that although uniform in many instances, would vary from one major site to another.

The Climb to Temple I

Temple I was constructed around 700 A.D. to commemorate one of the kings of the dynasty reigning in Tikal, "Pata de Jaguar." It is 145 feet high and at the top of the stairway is the temple itself. The upper part of the temple has what is called a "roof comb" which in this case was really a carved image of a seated individual in highly ornamental dress; but weather and age have practically destroyed the image.

This would be an altogether different and frightening experience for the young professor. The stairway is narrow, each step only a few inches wide and rather steep. The tourist hangs onto a metal chain placed in the middle of the stairway and proceeds to climb. The temple is 42.7 meters high; that translates to 145 feet or 15 to 20 stories high. It is one of the few pyramid temples at Tikal that also served as a tomb, in this case of the important king called "Jaguar Paw," thus the temple with the name "Temple of the Giant Jaguar." I could not look either to the side or in back of me as I climbed or vertigo would set in. I said to myself, "Just look straight ahead and climb; just look at the step in front of you." In fact I got along best when doing just that, concentrating the gaze on the stair in front of my face, the next step to climb. I was indeed weak in the knees by the time I reached the top, feeling a bit dizzy. I crawled as far as possible back away from the edge of the stairway, even back into the entrance to the temple on the top of the pyramid. I could scarcely move for a few minutes and just stayed close to the wall and away from the stairway. (Shades of Mel Brooks' film "High Anxiety!") The students did not seem nearly so frightened. I was dirty, tired, sweaty and dizzy.

The View Looking to Temples II, III, and IV

After a bit I became more used to it and actually began to enjoy the tremendous view: looking to Temple II across the plaza, the Acropolis to one side, Maler's Palace to the left. High off to the left one could see in 1976 Temple V, only the roof comb in sight above the jungle vegetation. And far away, straight ahead, beyond Temple II, one spied the tops of Temples III and IV.

The worst was yet to come—climbing down. I was fearful as one might surmise (shades of the time when I was very young on the farm near Abilene, Kansas, and had climbed onto the roof of the big old hay barn, and then had sat there for perhaps an hour or two before getting the nerve to get back on the rickety ladder. And it was only perhaps ten feet to the ground.) This fear of temples and their stairways would not disappear with time; the reader will hear more at Palenque, Uxmal, and especially Chichén-Itzá. But back to Temple I at Tikal, I finally was able to accomplish the descent in this way: I edged to the edge of the stairway, moving sideways like a crab, turned around to face the temple doorway, grabbed on to the chain and put my knees and posterior over the edge down to the first or second stair. Hanging on for dear life, I slowly made my way down, once again looking only at the step immediately in front of me. As I wrote later, in the end it seemed to be a matter of saving face. All the students had done it; could Herr Director do any differently? There would have been great regret otherwise, but I am sure the topic received an epic telling amongst the students over beers and laughter.

Should an interested tourist read these pages and relate to them and me, it will all have been worth it. I have known terror, real terror, only a time or two in life; this was one of those moments.

Less fearful but almost as impressive was the climb up Temple II, a pyramid just slightly smaller than Temple I. It is of approximately the same time frame as Temple I but is less tall, some 124 meters in size. It is noted for the temple on top that is decorated with "graffitos" or drawings done by hand of various Maya symbols, including one of a dead man with a lance through his chest. The wooden roof beam or "dintel" that was in place at the entrance to the temple is today in the Museum of National History in New York City; it depicts a figure of a Maya noble, perhaps a woman, dressed ornamentally in a long dress with a large image of Tlaloc, the god of rain of Teotihuacán. The view looking out from the front of the temple entrance is outstanding—the view of Temple I and the jungle beyond.

The North Acropolis—the Central Acropolis

The North Acropolis begun probably around 200 B.C. contains the tombs of the principal rulers of those times. The tombs themselves are buried under successive new temples of the Acropolis, these reconstructed at the death of each ruler. Many of the stelae and artifacts in the Museum of Tikal were found in this Acropolis. In the same complex is what they call "The Mask of Tlaloc," the god of rain of the central "meseta" of México, of Teotihuacán and later on the Toltecs. It is s just one among many objects which prove the early link between the two cities of Teotihuacán and Tikal.

Sweating profusely in the sun, we rested for a while and then moved on to the Central Acropolis, first looking at a very small ball court of Tikal (the tiniest I would see in Central America). There are three courts in Tikal, this being the largest. There are no rings on the walls as at Chichén-Itzá or markers as in Copán. Experts say the game was played by three players on each side; they could "hit" the hard rubber ball with their chest. This explains in the few "proofs" that exist that the players wore a sort of "pechero" or chest protector, probably of thick cotton. The belief that the games were "to the death," with the sacrifice of the losing players, is a concept not proved at least in the case of the ball game at Tikal.

There are many buildings in the Central Acropolis, and "Maler's Palace" is among them. The latter is the temple where the researcher Maler lived for several months while excavation took place in 1890. I believe both he and his clothes would have been a bit moldy from the experience (like my green suit hanging in the armoire in Recife in Brazil's tropical northeast for six months, turning a light grey). There were graffiti as we saw in Temple II and places where water was supposedly gathered after rainstorms and stored. Both the Petén and Yucatán have a limestone base as I understand it; water seeps quickly through the thin soil, so it had to be conserved, perhaps by an application of clay in a sort of "tank" surrounded by low walls. One can only imagine the mosquitoes that this would have engendered. One of the extant theories to explain the end of the classical period and Mayan culture is indeed that prolonged drought had brought its demise.

The buildings in the Central Acropolis contained many temples, and the ones excavated were in the style of classic Mayan architecture. The key to it all is the corbeled arch, not a true rounded arch as those of the Arabs and Romans, but an arch dependent on a "capstone" to support the two walls. A series of such arches, all built together, allowed for the temple, the interior room and roof beams included. The problem is that it greatly restricted the size of the rooms.

An aside: as long time summer residents of Colorado and the Four Corner area, we are justly proud of our own Pre-Colombian heritage, i.e. the Anasazi cultures at Mesa Verde, Hovenweep, Chimney Rock and Chaco Canyon in New Mexico. The scientists are divided once again as to why the Anasazi cliff dwellings were abandoned around 1100 A.D; one theory is that there was warfare, but another, perhaps just as likely, is that a long, prolonged drought hit the area. Hence, one understands the comparison with the Mayan Classic Period sites.

After climbing through several levels we reached the top of the Central Acropolis where lo and behold there was a nice breeze, an immense relief from the stifling heat below.

Mark and the "Bat" Stela in the "Plaza Mayor"

I add an interesting note in regard to some of the stelae in front of the North Acropolis. Stela 4 is different in that it does not show the figure in profile, but directly ahead, as in a portrait. It shows the complete face of a warrior, in the style of Teotihuacán, with a headdress depicting a jaguar (some say it represents a bat, a god of the night) with a necklace of shells. One notes that these stelae were done without the use of metal; stone was sculpted with other stones or rocks, probably obsidian.

Temple IV

Students Climbing Through Tree Roots Up to Temple IV

The group was then bused to the site of Temple IV. This time I did not make the trip to the top, too tired and hot I thought. There was in 1976 a series of large tree roots at the base; you scramble up and through them and end up on a path and eventually get to the excavated part of the temple. (The next year I will do this temple justice.) In 1976 Keah climbed the temple; Mark did not. While waiting for the folks climbing Pyramid-Temple IV to come down, Mark took a path through the nearby forest, thick and tropical. Among other things, I watched long lines of leaf cutter ants that had stripped leaves from trees and were carting them to their subterranean home. The leaves were much larger than the ants, but all were marching along in perfect and continuous order, a sight I had only seen in National Geographic films. One can only recall the short story "Lonegan and the Ants" and the movie version with Charlton Heston if I am not mistaken—a frightening story of migration of the huge ants of the Amazon and the hero Charlton Heston's battle against them. I highly recommend the movie for a scary, good time. It's in the archives somewhere.

Round Altar 5, a Close-up

Near Temple IV was the famous, round Altar 5 along with Stela 16, both seemingly "planted" in the middle of the trail. This altar has glyphs in a circle all around it as well as the dots and bars indicating the time the work was done, and in the center are two figures. Are they priests, nobles, or warriors? All are in fine, classic garb and are kneeling before a skull and bones. The face of the skull is defaced as usual as on most of the stelae and other images at Tikal. The reason for the defacing was never explained convincingly to me, whether vengeance by conquerors or whatever. Modern day anthropologists say that the contemporary natives' dislike of tourist cameras may be related: the photo may "capture" their spirit! This altar, say the archeologists, proves the existence of human sacrifice at Tikal. And this in turn brings up a serious, long debated subject: this entire question of human sacrifice. An aside is to be permitted (better to deal with it now than later).

For many decades in the 20th century, and really from beginnings in the 19th, the Mayan Civilization was thought of as more "civilized" and certainly less blood-thirsty than that of their much later on neighbors the Aztecs in Mexico. Scholars called them "the Greeks of America" and the Aztecs "the Romans." The former were thought of as peace loving, a nation of "philosopher-priests." They were judged to be beyond the concept of human sacrifice. As time has passed, the glyphs deciphered and more evidence unearthed, literally, it is now accepted that indeed they practiced war, and war of conquest, and that prisoners were taken and sacrifice took place. In fact it became known that the greatest sacrifice was the blood-letting of the king himself. The dripping of blood from his penis on sacred "paper" which was subsequently burned produced smoke rising to the heavens. The smoke was understood as prayer or supplication to the gods, and his was the greatest "sacrifice." I always have found the use of incense in Roman Catholic services to be, ironically, of similar import.

The "Posada de la Selva"

Keah, John Cassidy outside the "Posada de la Selva"

After all the above, we were back to the "Posada de la Selva" for a lunch of meat, rice, salad and semi-cold beer. Tired, we wandered about and went over to the casitas where some of the students who had opted to stay the night would stay. In passing, it is necessary to mention the small, but excellent museum on the site: it possessed fine stelae and ceramics of the classic period. The museum has a replica of the tomb found under Temple I, replete with skeleton and jade jewelry.

After lunch, only a short distance away from the airstrip, an incredibly stifling hot airplane interior awaited us before takeoff. There were no fans or air conditioning while we waited. After revving up the engines to the max and undertaking an agonizing run down the runway, from the plane we saw the line of trees approaching. We all rooted (silently I think and perhaps in the form of informal prayer but without blood sacrifice) for lift off; the plane did just that and barely skimmed the trees for a rough flight back to Guatemala City.

In 1977 there was a reprise to Tikal, but on this second visit Keah would remain at the "Hogar," not wanting to risk any problems with air craft pressurization and the physical strain of being at the ruins, this due to her pregnancy with our future daughter Kathleen. But there are a few new stories to be told.

TIKAL: THE VISIT OF 1977

The plane in 1977 was an old DC-4 of Aviateca airlines.

Howler Monkey Swinging Through the Trees

This time we saw howler monkeys in the trees behind Temple II; they were harvesting the fruit dropping from the trees. Both the sight and the sound were impressive.

And this time Mark climbed to the top of temple IV with the twisted roots and vines as a ladder at the bottom. He sat with young students Flip, Cindy, Maggie and Keith admiring the impressive view from the top: the dense jungle and the tops of Temples I, II and V in the distance. And there was a pleasant surprise: a very nice, cool breeze up on top, quite a contrast to the stifling heat down below.

This time I spent the night at the "Jungle Inn." My room was in one of the "long houses," in effect a small cubicle, among many, with a wooden partition about three feet high serving as a wall on all four sides, and above it a "chicken wire" divider. The screen was rotten and full of holes; the door had no lock on it, and the bathroom was outside the long house, down the way, and not a nice place to visit. The latter came into play later that night after much beer and talk with the students in the p.m. at the Lodge. After the beer, we all retired to our rooms. I slept like a log for two hours, but then had to use the facilities. Did I mention that not unexpectedly there was no electricity at the "Jungle Inn," the result of a generator that they turned off very early in the evening. I had no light or flashlight. In the absolute darkness I could not find the matches for the candle they provided us with "room service." I heard noise, a kind of "whirring" sound. When I found a match on the floor beside the bed and struck one, I discovered the floor of the room and the walls were entirely covered with insects of all kinds. So I "crunched" my way out the door to the bathroom and ever so reluctantly returned to the darkness and my bed to while away the hours until dawn.

Temple I, the "Plaza Mayor" Through the Morning Fog

Notwithstanding the scene just described, the forest, the ruins, the birds and animals made it all worthwhile. Perhaps the highlight of this was the next morning. Several of us got up at 5:15 for an early walk to the ruins. We walked to the gate, which is coincidentally also the entrance to the Uaxactun Road. Inside the main site shortly before dawn, I found myself sitting on the roof of Maler's palace in the Acropolis when there was a sudden, huge racket of what seemed like screeching. It was bird noise: flights of parrots above the ruins, an unforgettable scene and memory both for sight and sound—seeing the birds and Temple I through the fog and mist of dawn. One thinks later, "How I would like to witness this again!" One sometimes realizes, it may never happen!

The rest of the visit was really very similar to what has already been described in 1976. After a rough flight home, it was good to be with Keah once again at the "Hogar."

ROUTINE AT UNIVERSIDAD FRANCISCO MARROQUÍN AND DAYS IN GUATEMALA CITY

Returning to the routine of the summer of 1976, the next day was Sunday, June 6. We went to mass at the old Santo Domingo church, the cathedral of Guatemala City, and had the "suerte" of hearing a long-winded priest. Back at the pensión for lunch I began a diet of soup, bread, and eggs "por pura necesidad." The antibiotic they eventually gave me for what was alluded to as "amoebic dysentery" had a warning in small print on the label. I swear—it said that taking for a period of time might cause blindness! Sounded like Russian Roulette to me. For something to do, a distraction of sorts, we took bus n. 13 later that p.m. for an hour and one-half ride through the poorest parts of the city, including the "barrios" or slums of those left homeless by the earthquake. The only change was when we reached the upscale part of the city near Avenida Reforma and one part near the zoo. The bus returned via 6a.Avenida and stopped at San Francisco church, also very damaged by the quake. Our ride included the run past the National Police Building. Back in 1962 I had a friend from Rockhurst University, one Rodolfo Contreras, whose father was chief of police of Guatemala at the time.

There were incessant rains throughout these days.

Monday. School. Good classes. Some of the students are still in Tikal. Keah and I after classes made a visit to the Center of Folkloric Studies at the Universidad Autónoma de Guatemala. One might recall that my dissertation days in Brazil were very involved with folklore. The director here in Guatemala, Professor Castillo, seemed to take a complete Marxist view of folklore.

Tuesday. Good 'ole bus n. 2 would not stop for us near the "pensión," so we took n. 4 that followed up 7a. Avenida to the Civic Center. From there we walked to the university, fortunately past the incredible Iglesia del Sagrado Corazón (which reminded me a bit of Gaudí's in Barcelona which I knew only from pictures). Then we went to the folklore center at the Universidad de San Carlos where I met Licenciado Roberto Díaz Castillo who gave me several of the publications of the Center. It reminded me very much of the way the Center for Folklore in Rio de Janeiro worked under its director, Dr. Renato Almeida. Very pleasant in demeanor, Professor Castillo seemed well in control and most of the publications seemed to have his finger on them.

Next day. Keah and I have been thinking of taking off (alone!) to go to Lake Atitlán for the weekend. I hope so. Vera the secretary has helped us greatly through the ordeal of directing the day to day of the summer school. The textbooks are finally here; the atmosphere in the pensión is better now, and the students have made more contacts and friends and are simply more accustomed to Guatemala. But we could still use a break!

After lunch we took the bus downtown, first to the Banco de Londres y Montreal to see the great murals, and to cash some travelers' checks. Then we took bus n. 1 to Parque Minerva to see the famous relief map of Guatemala. It indeed is unique and perhaps good for one visit. There then was a "paseo" through the park, all very green with lots of flowers at one end where one sees a large "barranca," cliff or canyon. The return was past the tourist commission, the "Regional" store and a great German pastry shop on 11a. Calle called "Los Tilos."

The Next Day. We missed Bus n. 2 again so we took n. 13 and there ensued a ride through the suburbs before arriving late once again to school. There would be an outing with Professor Juárez Paz that p.m. which turned up something important. We went to the "Archivo Nacional" behind the National Library where in a badly illuminated room we saw the original manuscript of Bernal Díaz del Castillo's "La Verdadera Historia de la Conquista de Nueva España." Bernal Diaz had retired in Guatemala after the heady moments of the conquest of the Aztecs in 1521. Important stuff this was! It is one of the major reports of the conquest of Mexico, that by the "common soldier." The book is on the reading list, the required one, for study of the Conquest of Mexico.

Boys Just Want to Have Fun, Bill in the Dryer

A funny tourist-student aside: after the morning outing, a rather pedestrian moment took place. We went up 7a. Avenida and Reforma to the only laundromat in that part of the city. There Bill, one of my favorite students, is captured in film while doing a bit of a whirling act in a dryer. Then it was back to the "pensión" for beers (el Gallo), cigars and good times with the students. Ethel, one of the stalwart young ladies, helped cook supper-"Arroz Valenciano-" "Sabrosa estuvo la cena."

A school note from the Next Day: On bus n. 1 to UFM there was chaos and we were packed like sardines inside; many passengers were arguing with the driver. Spanish 201 Class at school did not bring good vibes, but Civilization was okay with the Incas.

In the p.m. we took bus n. 2 to the Iglesia de Nuestra Señora de las Angustias. The architecture is a mixture of arabesque and who knows what else. The beautiful wooden carvings inside are outstanding.

There were other outings in Guatemala City. One was to the "Jardín Botánico" which was pretty, fresh and somewhat similar to that in Rio de Janeiro, but smaller. Then there was a "Paseo" on Avenida Reforma past the "Escuela Superior de Guerra" with the cadets in their green and red uniforms. The ride took us past the local embassies and their gardens, but alas, one sees very little of the inside of such places due to the high, protective walls around them.

Next day at UFM. We experienced another crisis with one of the young female students; her family wants to throw her out of the house. Professor Juárez—Paz and Secretary Vera are exasperated. I succeeded in asking everyone to cool off and wait a few days.

A SAVING OUTING: THE FIRST TRIP TO "EL LAGO DE ATITLÁN" AND CHICHICASTENANGO

The tension alluded to earlier was readily resolved with the next outing, a wonderful experience!

Lake Atitlán-an Introduction

It was this lake than helped kindle my immense love for the country of Guatemala. I was introduced to it for the first time in 1962 where I had a wonderful initial experience told in the "preamble" of this book, another fine visit in 1969 after a year's work in Brazil, a brief visit of tourism, in effect part of a "second honeymoon" with wife Keah, and finally, more extensive stays during the summer schools of 1976 and 1977.

The Lake is landlocked with no rivers or other openings to the sea, although scientists have long thought there was an underground flow to the Pacific. The water level did drop a full two meters after the devastating earthquake of 1976, but no one has pinpointed the exact cause. It is a clear, cold water lake at about 340 meters of depth. It was formed as the "caldera" of a volcano long ago and today has three major volcanoes surrounding it to the south, the Volcán Atitlán, Volcán San Pedro and Volcán Tolíman. Intensive fishing has lessened over the years, but Black Bass at one time populated the lake and were a source for food for the natives as well as sport fishing.

There are twelve indigenous towns surrounding the beautiful lake, or there were, for volcanic activity and a massive flood have taken a heavy toll on them. These and the greatest problem of all—man himself. In the 1980s the right wing military government in Guatemala in a "scorched earth policy" attacked natives by the lake unmercifully, killing hundreds and driving many away forever. It was "war against Communists and subversives." There are still machine gun bullet holes on the buildings of Sololá above the lake. In spite of all this, the fields and embankments all around the lake contain extremely rich volcanic soil and the natives farm it intensively, mostly a sort of truck farming of vegetables, but much corn as well.

The towns which are not all named here include Sololá above the lake, Panajachel at the bottom of the major road down into the lake, at times a hippy haven, but always a vacation spot for the wealthy from Guatemala City, and many other towns. The largest and best known across the lake is Santiago Atitlán, home incidentally to the best known Indian deity worshiped in the folk religion of the area, Maximón. Others are Santa Catarina Palopó and San Antonio Palopó and San Pedro de la Laguna. Each village is known for unique and spectacular weaving with its own colors, patterns and themes. The languages of the natives are Tz'utuhil and Cakchiquel.

It is possible to take a tourist boat across the lake to Santiago Atitlán (some call it the mail boat) but natives will also provide taxi service in their dugout canoes or "cayucos" for a price. But everyone knows that the beautiful lake is treacherous as well with the famous "xocomil" or violent, high water in the p.m. Many lives have been lost.

Finally, in these villages one has the opportunity to see unspoiled, legitimate Indigenous religious customs still practiced.

For these reasons and for the time spent there with my good Guatemalan friend Eduardo Matheu and his family, and for the wonderful times shared there with my wife Keah, it is still one of my favorite spots on the planet.

The "Unofficial" ASU Outing to the Lake in 1976

The ASU "official" trip did not "make," so this outing was arranged just for a small group of us via Guatemala Sightseeing.

We met the students at UFM: Connie, Ann Clelland, Terri, John Cassidy, Bill Hale, Barbara Cortright, Keah and I. (The others were on their own, Lord knows doing what.) First stop was at the Inn on the way to the Lake—El Katok—for beer and sausage. Then we saw the ruins of Tecpán (I had been there years earlier on horseback with Eduardo Matheu and his nephews). So we passed right by my favorite place in Guatemala, the Vista Bella farm. Along the road we saw once again the small corn fields ("milpas") of the Indians and the small farms ("fincas"), beautiful indeed!

Sololá and View above the Lake

Students and Photo Op above the Lake

From up above the lake was entirely clouded in; there was fog and clouds in Sololá and on up, but as we traveled down the winding road to the lake, it cleared. Spectacular!

Keah at the Rancho Grande

Our group all stayed at the Rancho Grande, $10.75 for the night with breakfast. Señora Marlita was our host; she is the daughter of the German founder of the Inn, who in turn was a fishing buddy of Eduardo Matheu's father; the former drowned in the lake while on a fishing trip. Do not underestimate the "xocomil" or fierce p.m. waves on the lake! Our photos show the beautiful whitewashed cabanas of the Rancho Grande with thatch roofs, some with red tile, the inside furnishings of wood and the ceilings with dark, wooden beams. It all seemed a cross between the tropical and Bavaria. There was a luxurious lawn full of flowers, ferns, and some orchids. This inn is strictly upper class—Guatemalan Atitlán style!

Breakfast the next morning was eggs, toast, and wonderful pancakes with honey. The "dueña" María knows María Mertins of our residence in Guatemala City, the "Hogar." She told us of the boating accident where six fishermen, including her father, drowned. There are flowers and birds everywhere—"país tropical." We noted an Indian cutting the lawn with a machete!

Students at "El Cisne" along the Lake

Last Night. We were with all the students in a simple café down near the lake front—"El Cisne" (The Swan). It turned into a party with liters of beer and poor Basilio, a Mayan Indian and his family, trying to handle the horde of students, more business I think than they had had in months. For $1.25 each of us had a meal of soup, meat, vegetables, chile relleno, postre y café. Afterwards we repaired to the Rancho Grande and to the little house with the fireplace the students had rented and lots of "plática." We enjoyed the long varanda in front of our own place, the beautiful view of the other "casitas" and the garden area. The next day we sat there for two hours during an incredible tropical rain, high and dry and all beautiful. The traffic passing on the little street in front kept our attention—all manner of Indians back and forth with normal routines, carrying wood, down to the lake to fish, etc.

Saturday a.m. Keah and I were up quite early for breakfast and conversation with Marlita. Afterwards we then did one of the most pleasant outings I have done in Guatemala. Keah and I set out walking from El Rancho Grande on a fresh and beautiful morning, out of Panajachel, across a log bridge across the stream coming into the lake, through a wet, humid sector, and through a coffee plantation. Along the way we ran into little Indian ladies, always dressed in the local, woven clothing of the nearby village of Santa Catarina Palopó. At one point along the trail we climbed higher and could see the entire lake plus the three volcanoes surrounding it, a stunning view of San Pedro, Toliman and Atitlán. At this high point I walked off the beaten path on another quite muddy one, going straight up the mountain. It literally followed the paths through the cultivated fields on terraces on the side of the lake. The natives were planting onions by hand: they hoe the soil well, dig or punch a small hole with the end of the hoe, place a tiny onion seedling in and in one motion tamp the ground around it. The soil was dark, rich, good humus. The Mayan farmer told me they receive six to seven "quetzales" per thousand onions grown and harvested.

Maya Farmer Planting Onions on Slopes of Lake Atitlán

On up the slope I could see where they had hoed all the weeds and cleared the soil to plant "milpas," that is, corn. I am wondering how these small plots stand the erosion that must come with the incredibly hard tropical rains they get here. The farmer I talked to offered his son—Maximiano Tax Gómes—to accompany us to the town and find a dugout canoe ("cayuco") for the return trip to Panajachel, this for $1.50. So we continued the "paseo," now with young Max with us. Nearing Santa Catarina Palopó, yet some distance away, we heard music of marimba and clarinet, both instruments seeming "desafinados" or out of tune to each other. From above there was a pretty view of the town with its freshly painted, whitewashed church, a total absence of cars or trucks or any vehicle for that matter, the music echoing through the mountains, the fields and terraces above the town and lake, the volcanoes to the right. We were indeed the only outsiders in that place.

Once down into the town and heading toward the sound of the music, we climbed up one or two totally impoverished streets with poor huts with straw roofs on the side. Another matter: later I came upon a book by a University of Arizona author called "Campesino." It had stories of the Indians of Atitlán during the oppression of the 1970s and 1980s.

In the town we saw women weaving, the central "pila" or fountain, Indian women coming for water with large plastic jars on their heads (replacing the clay jars of years ago, heavier by far). All were in local dress.

The Façade of the Church of San Antonio Palopó

Images of Saints Lined up Inside the Church

The local church was unusual: the outside seemed brand-new, sparkling white on the façade with two lions of Spain painted in vivid colors. Inside all was a disaster from the recent earthquake; the images were all stacked in the front, most with native dress. The Virgin Mary, for example, appeared in the exact dress of the women of the pueblo with her "huipil" and beads.

Men and Boys Practicing Dances for Festival of Patron Saint

We climbed the streets to the place where the men were practicing for a feast day in town; the music was humble and poor, the men were practicing dance steps, all in a muddy, filthy area between very poor huts. It is a cliché to be sure, but we did witness a true slice of life of the village that day, pure and unadulterated by the outside world.

Big and Little Sister along the Shore

Fixing Dugout Canoe, Lake Atitlan

Back down by the lake there were more gardens, men tending their "cayucos" and ladies doing the wash and also giving baths to their children.

Indians with Pigs on Way to Market in Sololá

We were going to return by "cayuco," but the "xocomil," wind, high waves and stormy clouds before rain, had begun, so we decided to return on foot. On the way we saw Indians with large hogs on tethered ropes; they were going to walk them all the way to the market of Sololá above the lake. I have a picture of a chicken roosting on top of one of the heavy hoes.

All in all, it was a memorable experience for us, beautiful. In spite of the social system in Guatemala in 1976, the poverty and the misery, that morning and that walk were beautiful. Not even the worst of social evils can take away the view, the smells, the sounds, the purity of nature and the crops in those fields, the lake, the volcanoes, and the quiet dignified ways of the Indians we talked to. I have always maintained that in spite of all social evils, there is a beauty and dignity to the native peoples of Guatemala which I hope never disappears.

We returned to the Rancho Grande for a rest and an "almuerzo" in El Cisne with Indians hawking their weavings outside the door. There followed a siesta in the Rancho Grande accompanied for two or three hours of tremendous rain. We were wrapped up in ponchos on the veranda taking it all in. Indians were constantly passing using plastic sheets for raincoats, all about their normal business.

Once again we had dinner that evening at El Cisne with the students; there were beers, lots of laughter and joking. Later someone gave us "un jalón," a "hitch" to the Hotel Monterrey where student Bill Wyatt was having a birthday party. The ole' professor played the guitar a bit that night. It was like the old days, Mark playing for his sweetheart!

The Trip to Chichicastenango

Introduction

Chichicastenango, a name supposedly given to the town by the Spanish conquistadors' allies from Tlaxcala in Mexico, a Naháutl name, is the capital of the Department of Quiché in the highlands of Guatemala. It is a mountain town at about 6500 feet, surrounded by what is left of pine forests and with dense "mini-fundia" agriculture by the Indians surrounding the place. Its claim to fame is as a regional marketplace for the Indians but "adopted" by the hordes of tourists who visit Guatemala.

The town center in front of its major church, Santo Tomás de Chichicastenango, is a thriving, busy market place two times a week and should not be missed by anyone wishing to see the colors, religious practices but also the poverty of the highlands Indians.

The Church of Santo Tomás is the cultural highlight of town because the space below it is linked to pre-Colombian times and was a religious site for the Quiché Indians. In fact the 18 steps leading into the church reflect the 18 months of the pre-Columbian Maya calendar. The scene is totally syncretistic, that is, Mayan and Catholic. The highlight for the tourist is to quietly, calmly and respectively, sit in an old wooden pew and observe the Maya rites: shamen or "curanderos" practice as well as many ladies, all bringing their candles and their "aguardiente" or soft drinks as aids in the many prayers and rituals practices.

The high end traditional tourist place in town is the Maya Inn, lodging and restaurant for the tourists. But the highlight for most folks is the incredible opportunity for bargaining and purchasing of beautiful woven products. The town is known as well as a major producer of the wooden masks used in various Mayan rites in Guatemala.

The Trip Diary

After a good breakfast we traveled by VW Van to Chichicastenango in the rain on a narrow road through the mountains with terraced fields alongside.

At one point there was a funeral with men carrying a carved wooden casket along the road.

Chichicastenango and the Market.

It was impressive for the really large number of Indians there that day, many more than I had seen on previous trips, and of course it was full of tourists. The whole thing seemed to be a big mud puddle. The Iglesia de Santo Tomás was impressive as ever—and dangerous—propped up with timbers since the earthquake of February of the same year.

Members of the "Cofradía" or Religious Brotherhood Entering the Church

The leaders of the "cofradías" or "hermandades," religious brotherhoods that is, paraded in and out of the church with their ceremonial clothing, including the "tzut" or headdress of woven cloth in beautiful woven patterns. (In fact I bought one and it decorates the wall of our living room in Mesa.) All were carrying ornate silver staffs which reminded me of monstrances of silver.

Indian Ladies and Shamen "Curanderos" Praying inside of Santo Tomás

There were more Indians than ever inside the church. The Indians were worshiping. Evidence of this were candles burning, flower petals and corn placed around the burning candles, and the occasional sprinkling of "huaro" or "aguardiente" on the flames by the priests while chanting or praying in probably "cakchiquel."

We particularly watched one Indian who we think was a shaman heading prayer and response.

After the really religious experience inside the church, we were a bit frustrated and tired with the shopping going on outside. The quality of the tapestries seemed not as good as in the past. Nor were the vendors as friendly as the Indians in Antigua, Guatemala City or even Atitlán. All seemed a big tourist business. I do believe that this is just the reality of modern day Chichicastenango.

After the market we made a quick visit to the Mayan Inn (I recalled the place from visits in 1962 and 1969). It was beautiful with its colonial trappings, but was "out of place" to me with all the rich tourists and their drinks. But the colonial furniture, fireplaces and wooden balconies were a sight to see.

There was a quick trip to the animal market outside of town where we saw the natives with their hogs and sheep for sale.

THE RETURN TO GUATEMALA CITY

The return to Guatemala City was beautiful; there was a stop at Katok for sausages in tortillas. We arrived in the city on a clear, pretty afternoon, the city air cleansed by showers of rain. I said to myself, "Thank God for the weekends and the trips."

In Guatemala City at the Santo Domingo Church there were people camped in tents living on the grounds in front of the church due to the quake. They moved the statue of the Virgin and the Christ "laying down" into a nearby building.

María Mertins' daughter at the pension is a prima ballerina and has a studio across the street from the "pensión."

Later on there was a visit to San Francisco church with an anthropologist who explained the efforts at preservation after the earthquake: the tombs contained bones mixed up with the quake and they were using epoxy trying to glue it all back together.

TRIP TO THE PACIFIC AND PUERTO SAN JOSÉ

The Group to the Pacific at Amatitlán

Up at 5:45! We drove to Lake Amatitlán and then to Palín whose plaza had the largest "La Ceiba" tree in all Guatemala. Legend: it was planted by the Conquistador Alvarado's wife 400 years ago. Then as we headed toward the Pacific and descending from the highlands, there were huge loaded trucks of sugar cane and sugar cane fields to the side of the highway. We saw green pastures with lots of cattle and bananas and papaya trees. And also immense poverty.

People on Black Sand Beach at Puerto San José

Beached Cargo Ship at Puerto San José

The tourist van proceeded on to the Pacific and resort of Chulamar. It seemed expensive to the students and us so we continued on and went to the public beach at San José. The sand was black, the result of volcanoes. At Pier 4 we saw tugs and small boats hauling cargo to ships off shore and vice versa, the reason being is that there is no natural bay for docking at San José. In fact we encountered a huge beached ship from Monrovia in South Africa; it had been too expensive to try to pull it off the beach. We experienced rain and volcanoes, one smoking, on the way back to Guatemala City.

A SECOND TRIP TO ANTIGUA AND SAN ANTONIO ÁGUAS CALIENTES

Keah says, "Green, green"—young corn plants seem like spiders coming out of the ground! We take the long route through Chimaltenango to get to Antigua due to mudslides and the fact that the quake had destroyed the main road. Once in Antigua we went to San Francisco church for mass. Some people at mass were wearing a rope around their waist, like a scapular. After mass, many of the Indians gathered, built a communal fire outside the church and cooked.

We then saw ruins of old Santa Clara convent (this was the convent I had visited in 1962 with friend Eduardo Matheu where his aunt was one of the nuns).

Moving on, it was a feast day at San Antonio Águas Calientes. I just recall having to sit on a board seat in the bus and seeing the destroyed church. Its images were temporarily housed in a wooden building to the side. It housed separate little shrines for each image of a saint.

Part of the festival was seeing four, tall giant women made from frames out of wood and with gingham dresses. They were carried in a parade: two white girls, two black, one with a machete. Many Indians were in town for the festival; there were typical foods; the women were in "huipiles."

The rains came again and there was some flooding, so we hopped the bus back to Guatemala City. I don't know if I mentioned before, but Keah and I were on our own this time. "This is like the bus trips in Colombia," says Keah.

The next week brought student John Cassidy's birthday party with music and food, and Mark played the guitar (for Keah, I think we are still in love!).

There is an official outing to Professor Juarez Paz's farm or "finca." I recall the forest, fields of corn, lunch, orange groves, and cattle. Perhaps most striking was when they pointed out an earthquake fault line.

THE TRIP TO COPÁN, HONDURAS

An Introduction to Copán

The archeological zone of Copán has been known since 1576. It is the "religious center" of one of the largest Maya cities from the Classical Period which flourished from the 4th century A.D. The ruins are situated in the western part of the Republic of Honduras and the capital of this department is called Santa Rosa de Copán. The town is just one kilometer from the ruins and has 3000 inhabitants; it is a modern and tranquil place.

Of all the great cities founded by the Maya, Copán was the first to be known, but we don't know exactly when and by whom. It is doubtful that the conquistadors arrived at this place. The first news we have of Copán is in 1576 when a member of the "Real Audiencia de Guatemala" described the site to King Felipe II in a letter. Three centuries passed before the next notice in 1834, and five years later the first expedition arrived at the site, that of John L. Stephens and Frederick Catherwood, the latter an artist from England, the former a North American diplomat. The book of travels of the two, "Incidents of Travel in Central America, Chiapas and Yucatan," is yet today a classic both for its commentary and its lithographs.

The origin of the name "Copán" is discussed and debated, but it is attributed to an Indian chief called Copán-Calel who battled against the Spaniards in the 19th century.

The most famous modern scientist-discover of the site is Dr. Sylvanus G. Morley, author of many studies on the Maya, who made various trips to the site and in fact became a "citizen-resident" of the town, paying taxes, etc. It was he who wanted to restore the site and obtained funds to do so from the Carnegie Institute.

Copán is in a small valley formed by the Río Copán which flows north into the Río Motagua which in turn flows into the Atlantic. The principal agricultural products of the region are corn, beans and squash, not to mention the tobacco which came later. The tobacco comes from Cuba, much of it planted since 1959 and the Castro regime when large tobacco farmers fled the island, but with seeds in hand.

The oldest stela is from 465 A.D. and the last from 800 A.D. The site of Copán was known for its science and its arts, for the abstract astronomical calculation for the Maya calendar, for its sculpture and their glyphs. The principal site consists in patios, stelae, small pyramids, temples and the acropolis. The most significant works are indeed the stelae, the altars, the ball court, the hieroglyphic stairway, the temples and the sculptures. They denote sixteen successive kings in the dynasty. Like Tikal, Calakmul and other sites, it was a religious center governed by a royal king, with nobles, warriors, artisans and slaves below him. One of its amazing stelae depicts the ascent to the throne of 18 Rabbit, his head coming out of the jaws of the earth monster, thus relating the king to the rising sun.

In a related matter, the classic city of Quiriguá, a rival of Copán and located fifty kilometers to its north, was known for the tallest and some of the most ornate of all Maya stelae. The site originally depended on Copán, but it was liberated from Copán's power when a Quiriguá King defeated 18 Rabbit at Copán, and then the city enjoyed one hundred years of its own success. The last date in Quiriguá is 810 AD. It has the tallest Maya stelae, one at an amazing height of eleven meters done in 771 AD and showing the king standing on a mask of the earth monster depicted as a jaguar.

Among monumental highlights of Copán are the Plaza Mayor with its many stelae, the Ball Court, the Hieroglyphic stairway and many other temples. Of note in more recent times was the discovery of "Rosalilla," the figure on the side on a pyramid which was covered over by the construction of yet another pyramid on top of it. The experts still wonder why the Mayas did not destroy "Rosalilla" as was the custom of the times, destroying previous constructions at the death of the king and building new ones for his sucessors.

The Trip with the Students in 1976

The Thatch Hut in the Countryside

Bill McPherson was the gracious driver; he teaches at UFM. There were a total of ten of us in a van setting out from Guatemala City. Soon after leaving the city and heading to the east, we saw a major bridge down from the quake. The road bed had shifted about 3 feet, its center line off 3 feet. We shortly thereafter saw what is called a volcanic plug; lava that never came out of the volcano cooled inside the volcano and naturally hardened. Gradually the rest of the volcano wore away and what is left is the hardened lava in the shape of a plug. Small country towns were common and also native local "chozas" or huts all of straw.

The Fruit Fly Fumigation

After driving through beautiful tropical settings we arrived at the Honduran border. There was time for a short siesta while we waited for the Honduran border crossing official dubbed "Happy Jack" because he smiled the whole time he "fleeced the tourists." Eventually, after much waiting, our tourist cards were stamped for a fee to allow us to leave Guatemala and enter Honduras. The van also suffered a bit of humiliation: it was fumigated in a cloud of smoke, supposedly to wipe out a nasty fruit fly suspected of carrying Guatemalan papers. We finally arrived at the town of Copán Ruinas at 4 p.m. There was time to see the Copán museum in town.

Hotel Marina in Santa Rosa de Copán

We stayed at the very modest Hotel Marina right off the town square where Professor Mark discovered vendors who sold six tiny cigars for 5 centavos. Mark and some of the students lit up, and no one turned green but all felt a bit queasy. There is a story to the cheap cigars of what turns out to be very fine tobacco. When Fidel Castro took over Cuba in 1969 and a few months later declared himself to be an avowed Socialist, many rich landholders got out while they could. Some of them, growers of Cuba's famous tobacco for those expensive cigars, migrated to Honduras and some to the Copán Valley. The soil is volcanic, incredibly rich, and the tobacco crops in some cases "improved" on the Cuban product.

That night during a magnificent tropical evening with cool breeze, Mark and a Honduran fellow, I think a government official with something to do with archeological excavation at the site, traded songs on guitar in the plaza, this over cigars and beer. That night Keah said, "This is like Santa Fe de Antioquia" with its small town plaza and all of us feeling very safe.

We heard horses clip clopping on cobblestones outside the hotel at 4:30 a.m., loud firecrackers and then voices singing. It turned out to be a procession with everyone carrying a candle and men carrying the Image of Our Lady of Perpetual Help; it all ended in church with a recitation of the Rosary. One would have to thank Our Lady for the lack of sleep.

We were all up at 6 a.m. and walked to the ruins; a minor irritation was that some local kids had let air out of Bill's tires.

Copán Ruinas

The Main Plaza of Copán with Stelae

The first one sees is the "Jardín Paseo" to the ruins lined with many trees—the "Árbol del Casamiento." Then one enters the ruins proper and is dazzled by the ceremonial patio, really a quadrangular amphitheater. It is huge, and it is believed that the stairs surrounding the amphitheater where used as seats as in a stadium. In the huge patio there are stelae with altars in front of most of them. We understand that below each stela was a sort of a deposit in which religious offerings were placed: vases, ceramics, jade beads, and bones.

The Stelae of Copán

These give rise to the notion of Copán as the "Paris of the Maya World." They are of stone carved in low relief with "portraits of Kings" on two sides and the other sides bearing inscriptions with glyphs. Usually there is an altar in front of the stela. The stelae are monolithic, of a greenish stone called "andesite" and are from 3 to 4 meters in height. It is believed that the stelae were made each "katun" or twenty years, probably corresponding to a human generation. One scholar said, "Of all that is Maya, things are always much more than they are perceived." The stelae definitely fit into that category. They were magnificent and awe-inspiring.

Because the stelae are so varied and so famous, I submit my poor recollections and description of just a few examples of the same.

Stela of a Noble at Copán

Stela A. It represents a masculine figure, looking straight ahead, with an advanced social standing: the figure displays sandals, a sort of stocking, large ear plugs and a tall headdress with a mask of the sun at its apogee. The hands, crossed in a seemingly pious way, carry a scepter of authority. On the back side of the stela are various blocks of glyphs which indicate the date of the stela, in this case around 731 A.D.

Yet Another Stela of Another Noble at Copán

Stela C. It is the only one which has two human figures, "front" and "back," both masculine. One is decorated with large ear plugs and a headdress with a mask. The figure on the other side has a large beard. There is a series of 15 glyphs on each side. This stela is well preserved because for a long time it was buried. One can still see traces of red paint which was the color on all the stelae, the color red being sacred to the Maya. It is surmised that the two figures represent the same noble personage at different stages of life.

Stela of a Female Figure at Copá

Stela H. It is notable because it represents a feminine figure, the only one in Copán that represents a queen. She has a skirt of a jaguar pelt to her knees and on top of the skirt, a type of "over skirt" with spheres, perhaps of jade, and ornate sandals. She sports a large sash about her waist and has a scepter in her hands. She wears large ear rings or plugs and a type of helmet or headdress covered with quetzal plumes. On the other side of the stela (n. 49) there is a mask with the grotesque head of a bird; in the middle of the mask is the solar sun and at the base glyphs. In the "bóveda" in front of the stela were found objects of jade and gold, the first time in such a closed monument. It is thought the precious stones came from Panama or Colombia.

The Ball Court

The Ball Court at Copán and the Hieroglyphic Stairway

To the south of the huge central plaza with its stelae and altars is the Ball Court. The court was in the form of a capital I, closed at the north end by steps and stelae and open at the south end. There were three markers on the sides: they took the form of three parrot heads, round, and symbols of the "day sun." More ritual than game, the ball game symbolized the forces of life versus those of death. Thus it was not a sport, but with a religious character, and was only played by the noble class. It is believed it was played like the game in Mexico employed by the Aztecs and the Toltecs, but in this case with each team with five players and a large hard rubber ball. One could hit the ball with any part of the body except the hands, but the ball may have weighed upwards to three kilos; therefore the players wore special clothing or equipment to protect from the "blows."

Altar Q

Altar Q 1

Altar Q 2

Altar Q was placed below the ball court and the hieroglyphic stairway. It was square with each side having four human figures. The hat or headdress of each is distinct, and it is thought the altar represents the 16 kings of the dynasty of Copán. Another idea, debated over the years, was that the 16 figures were "scientists or mathematicians" representing a sort of meeting where the concept of the Zero was established. This latter view has been denigrated since the deciphering of the glyphs. Yet another idea bandied about is that the figures are figures of authority, and that this altar was important in the history of the Mayas marking the computation of the year in 365 days.

The Hieroglyphic Stairway

The Hieroglyphic Stairway

The Hieroglyphic Stairway represents the largest Maya inscription anywhere. There are 63 stairs or steps, each with sculpted glyphs. There is a total of 2,500 stone blocks. The problem is that the stairway was reconstructed by the anthropologists and archeologists after earthquakes which left the site severely damaged, and archeologists had no idea which was the "proper order" of each stone, each which had its own glyph. Work is still going on trying to straighten this out, and in a way the task symbolizes much of what we call the Mayan Civilization and excavation of the same, some 1200 years after its apogee. In the center of the stairway are five statues of figures seated on luxurious thrones and one large altar. In 1976 only 30 blocks had been deciphered; much more is known now. The stairway was constructed from 544 AD to 744 AD, over a period of 200 years.

The Río Copán and Rich Fields to the East of the Ruins

After viewing these major objects we saw other temples. To the east side of the area on a hill above the Copán River with beautiful agricultural plots below were several notable monuments. One was in the form of a jaguar with spheres which one surmises were at one time filled with jade, another, a monument to Venus, and yet another, a much more realistic carving of a human head.

The Student Umbrella "Sacrifice"

The Professor Joining the Fun

The Jovial Group in Copán—Good Memories

There was more, but these indeed come to mind and memory after seeing the slides taken that day.

The trip home was marked with rain and drunks on the road. It was good Bill had loose change and bills because he needed them to bribe the officials at the border, but all's well that ends well. It was a terrific trip.

RETURN TO GUATEMALA CITY AND THE FINAL DAYS OF THE SUMMER SCHOOL IN 1976

Mark was busy making final exams and doing travel preparation for Mérida in the Yucatán.

On one of the final evenings friends Eduardo and Kit came to see us; we were invited to go over to Eduardo's parents' house where Mark had a wonderful reunion with Ed's father and mother. I recall a painting of the family showing Eduardo's great grandfather as a young boy. Supper was at a big "churrasco" place with dessert at the Ritz Hotel. It was indeed a great reunion.

The following day marked a party at the Spaish Conversation teacher's house. Later we were with students at the pensión with many songs and beer.

VISIT TO TECPAN AND VISTA BELLA

    While Mark was giving final exams and grading the same, Keah packed for our short outing. Eduardo and Kit arrived, and with Keah and Kit in the front seat and Eduardo and Mark in the back in the Datsun shell, we took off on the road from the city. It was dark when we got to the farm. The main house came down in the quake, so Eduardo and his family were living in a small wooden house with no electricity or running water. They used kerosene lanterns and a Coleman lantern for light. One had to walk down to the old house for running water, but it was still partially flooded. A maid fixes all the meals, cleans, and does laundry. Kit took on the large task of baking all the bread and cakes. Basically, the old house is ruined. It is indeed a matter of perspective, and all is relative is life, but certainly this is evidence that upper class owners suffered from the quake as well as others, and their lives were equally in danger.

    One could see the volcanoes of Lake Atitlan from their farm house. While Eduardo conducted business at the flour mill on the farm, Keah and Mark walked along the stream dividing the valley near the old farm house, enjoying the green grass and the warm sun.

Eduardo, Kit, Harry and Apple Orchard, Vista Bella

At one point we all drove with Ed to the other farm, Los Pinos; Eduardo plans to earn a profit by growing garlic on it. We noted the Indians working the fields. We enjoyed a lunch of sandwiches and apples from the farm trees, an innovation Eduardo brought from school days at the University of California, Davis, where he studied horticulture and fruit production. Another endeavor was that Kit was developing a big bakery to sell goods in the city, a good idea and natural thing, keeping in mind that there was a flour mill on the property.

We then took off for the lake, picking up some things in Panajachel, and then driving through Santa Catarina Palopó to Eduardo's parents' house overlooking the lake. Mark now had a bad cold, but managed to play guitar a bit that evening which incidentally produced a beautiful sunset on the lake from the house.

Eduardo, Mark, the Beach at Atitlán

Mark, "Cayuco" Ride, Atitlán

The next day Eduardo and Mark snorkeled and there was a canoe ride for the professor. Then Eduardo, Mark and Keah drove into Panajachel for mass; the old church had been destroyed and this was a new small one, more like a chapel. It was full for the service with mainly Indians present; both men and women went to communion. Mark noted: "This was our best mass in Guatemala."

After mass in town we were back on the beach at the house. It turns out their neighbor has funded the Guatemalan sailing team for the Olympics. He and his family arrive in a helicopter to their lake house. That afternoon Keah got a ride in a "cayuco" or dugout canoe with the Indian owner doing the paddling, not an everyday occurrence for us.

The moods of the lake and the volcanoes and the weather are changing as the day goes on. I've mentioned the "xocomil" or treacherous waves of the lake in the afternoons.

Since Eduardo and Kit have to get back to the farm, they drove us to the Rancho Grande in Panajachel where we all had supper, and then Kit and Eduardo and Harry returned home. They had offered us the use of the house, but we said no, preferring to lodge at the Hotel in the village where we were incidentally told one had to be careful at night because of "ladrones" in Panajachel.

There was a nice walk the next a.m. to local businesses with quiet streets. It was good to be with just Keah. Indians were parading their saints once again. We had lunch at the "Cisne" where its owner Basílio talked of the quake and the daughter he lost in it. Outside the café there were Indian ladies from Santa Catarina and we bought stuff. We then spent some time hanging around the lake, watching Indians, and fishermen. The next a.m. we enjoyed the good weather; there was a quiet moment watching an Indian lady wash her hair and then her small daughter's. They both were in full woven finery.

The bus back to Guatemala City was a Pullman and Indians were on and off the whole way. Up close the Indians are poor; perhaps no with no shoes and worn clothing. There were a huge number of buses at the station in the city; we were glad to get back to quiet and the soft song of canaries of the "pensión."

LAST DAY AT THE UNIVERSITY

Mark turned in grades, talked to Professor Juárez-Paz and we enjoyed a final lunch with the Professor of Philosophy. Our favorite Guatemalan secretary Vera unfortunately was sick and could not attend. We talked business; I found the professor a bit inscrutable, hard to figure. But it looks like we will return next year.

The remainder of the day was spent on laundry and packing for the Yucatan tomorrow.

AVIATECA TO MÉRIDA AND ON TO UXMAL, THEN TO THE ATLANTIC COAST AND ISLA MUJERES

All was smooth with the Aviateca flight to Mérida, that is, except for a few moments when the small pink jet dodged huge thunderheads we could see out the window. Arrival in Mérida was smooth with paperwork at the airport.

Our hotel was "La Posada Toledo," a funny place in an old colonial house; the room was big if not fancy, but comfortable with efficient ceiling fans for the tropics. Plus it was quiet!

We walked in the heat to the bus station where we bought tickets for Uxmal. I wrote, "In the restaurants, the waiters seem to be surly; we will be glad to get out of Merida." But there was one pleasant moment when we sat in one of the local parks and enjoyed the music and folk dancing.

OUTING TO UXMAL

Images of this famous site will properly be placed in "Mexico," Volume II. This was but a short "uneducated" visit to the site for the first time. The terrain was flat and dry on the way with cactus and henequen plants everywhere; we passed many old haciendas which seemed broken down and poor.

The first stop was Kabah and then an enormous Maya arch over a roadway, possibly the stone road to Uxmal. Of note at Kabah: there was one whole façade of a building with "Chac Mool" images.

Uxmal was of course impressive; we climbed to the top of the big temple. In spite of the site's importance, I leave a more complete description to later in this narrative. Recall we were at the end of a strenuous, sometimes nerve-wracking, but rewarding summer of work and play. We craved sun, rest and the beach.

Then came an equally impressive trip to Chichén-Itzá, our first time; once again I will chronicle the site in some detail later in this narrative. This was followed by the return trip to Mérida and then R and R to come.

The unusual and fun part was a bus trip from Mérida to the Caribbean coast via local bus. Of note was the fact the bus driver arrived either tired or hung over and allowed his very young son, we presume, to drive all the way to the Atlantic Coast, a bit unnerving for us. (I can only recall the film "Oh Brother Where Art Thou" when the young boy with wooden blocks tied to the bottom of his shoes in order to reach the foot feed and the brakes drives our heroes safely out of a burning barn.) We reached the coast safely, had about one hour's wait, and then took the boat to our destination of Isla Mujeres. The place was incredibly beautiful, a repeat of the scene of the Isla San Andrés experienced a year earlier on the trip to Colombia. I recall only a bit of Isla Mujeres—the cabana with the thatch roof and ceiling fans (which were perfect for the climate), the swimming and snorkeling on the nearby beaches (where we got the mother of all sunburns), saw the local boys diving for lobsters, and recall the sidewalks decorated with huge conch shells. We snorkeled some, but had to deal with some strong currents. The return ride to the coast in the small boat revealed incredibly blue Caribbean water.

II. FRANCISCO MARROQUÍN
SUMMER SCHOOL IN 1977

It is not necessary to repeat the details of the day in and out routine, for most days and travels were a repeat of 1976. But I will write of any new things that marked the summer. The main change was that Keah was pregnant in her sixth month and although enthusiastic and helpful as usual, was limited to some of the activities. So what follows are the moments I judge to be of interest in those few weeks in a Guatemala still ravaged by the earthquake of 1976, but also on the road to recovery. Of note are the moments we were able to witness Indigenous festivals and life, perhaps what really draw people to Guatemala.

Trip to Atitlán 1977

We left early Saturday a.m. with a jovial group to the lake. The scenery was pretty as usual. We stayed at El Rancho Grande Inn and its delightful owner Merlita de la Riva whom we had met on several previous occasions.

The group went immediately to "El Cisne" for a big lunch: beer, tortillas and guacamole, soup, beef, green beans, papas, dessert, and coffee. The cost was $3.10 for the two of us. Then as per usual at this time of year in Guatemala came the heavy, heavy rain. The students spent time playing with the parrots in the Cisne kitchen. After a while it was back to Rancho Grande for a siesta with the sounds of birds. Then Keah and I repeated a "paseo" to the river as in 1976.

Procession of the Saints, Atitlán

On our return we saw the "Procesión del San Francisco el Pequeño." It was an all-Indian affair led by old men with Indian flutes and then a woman with incense burner in full Atitlán dress. An old man played marimba and others with drums kept a simple rhythm. They carried four statues: San Francisco de Atitlán, San Francisco el Pequeño, la Virgen (in Indian dress and with buck teeth) and Jesus. The statues were carried on wooden platforms by the Indians. The music was eerie, but peaceful and unique to Atitlán and Indians; it reminded a bit of the flute band at the archeological park of San Agustín in Colombia in 1975. It was altogether a very nice experience. I felt and sensed the quietness, the smell and flavor of the Indian religion here in Guatemala.

That feeling changed some after the procession to the church when the images were taken inside. Drunk Indians danced outside.

There was a reunion with the students when we met Bill W. and others for a brief time. We all ate dinner at the Hotel Galindo, a beautiful place with lousy food. We were home to sleep early but yours truly worried that party noise by students would wake up Doña Merlita; no problem she says.

The next day started with a great breakfast at the RG: "piña, panqueques, huevos y café." Then there was time before leaving to walk down to the lake and watch the fishermen and the ladies washing vegetables and then themselves. It was another delightful ending to days at El Lago de Atitlán, one of my favorite places in the world.

Keah and Mark Leaving Atitlán, 1977

Chichicastenango 1977

It was a very, very pleasant experience this time. The group arrived and went directly to St. Thomas church where we witnessed the praying of the "curanderos" and a Catholic priest joining them. Here is what I remember of La Iglesia de Santo Tomás' ritual. There were flower petals on the floor as offerings: white for marriage, rose for safe travel, red for good business, and green for sickness. Candles were lit for the deceased and for marriage. Long tubes of incense were wrapped in corn husks, blessed inside to be burned outside.

The Catholic priest reads a prayer in Spanish on a piece of paper given to him by the Indian—a prayer for the deceased. He will say mass later. There is a 1 quetzal offering. He also blesses corn, apples, etc. which will be planted later.

The Indians pray to Pascual Abaj and to a trio of saints: Santo Tomás, San Sebastián and San José. Ladinos or whites pray to a Cristo Negro in the other church across the plaza.

One native couple arrives; the wife is pregnant. They ask the "curandero" to pray for an easy birth and the baby. The girl appears to be about 15 years old.

Confession and the mass are in both Spanish and Cakchiquel Maya.

Then we spend two delightful hours on the steps outside the church "taking in" the market. The following photos describe the highlights.

Children and "Rebozos," The Market in Chichicastenango

Resting outside the Church

Young Mother, "Bebé," and Father in the Market

Men of Sololá in the Market

Women Conversing Amidst the Masks

While sitting on the steps, a loudspeaker was blaring asking for contributions for the restoration of the church. We sat on the steps for one hour and it was unforgettable! After a bit we were completely ignored by the Indians and I got absolutely fantastic candid shots of them: Indian men, women, children and scenes of the market.

The total effect is a much deeper appreciation of their lives on market day. I felt a bit like one of them: resting and just watching the world go by and enjoying the excitement of market day.

Painting n. 1 Maya Inn

Painting n. 2 Maya Inn

A good dinner at the Mayan Inn followed. In 1977 the Inn was of two stories, painted orange, and with marimba music.

Afterwards I bought a beautiful "tzut", the headdress of the men of the "cofradía," this only after some friendly but strenuous bargaining.

There was enjoyable talk and reminiscing with the kids on the way home. We arrived very tired and early to bed at the Hogar.

Trip to Tecpán, Vista Bella, 1977

Once again this was a reprise with good friends Eduardo, Kit and son Harry Matheu from Guatemala. We left the pension at 7 p.m. after a very "gringo" supper at Danny's Pancakes: hamburger, fries, chocolate malt. Keah and I were desperate for a change from the cuisine at the "Hogar," especially with my queasy as usual stomach.

We arrived late to the family farm of Vista Bella. It was cold with a strong wind. Drinks and talk. I slept in Eduardo's father's bed upstairs in the attic with my nose about 6 inches from the ceiling. It was a great old bed but icy under the covers; Eduardo said we used six blankets.

Their permanent house is under construction with extra steel reinforcement for anti-earthquake measures. There is a great view toward Atitlán and the volcanoes.

The next a.m. we walked to the village of Vista Bella for the official inauguration of the "new" town reconstructed since the quake by the Boy Scouts and the Quakers. It amounted to a small feast day. Colonel Echevarría of the Guatemalan Military, in charge of the national reconstruction committee, was there and represented the President.

There was talk of politics, the PD, the CD. Eduardo says one party represents the highlands' vote, the other the wealthy industrialists. The last election was won supposedly by fraud. Eduardo stands more with the middle sized and small farmers' interests.

We then met Pablo Duchez, a cousin of Eduardo, the one I rode out to the ruins of Iximché with in 1962; we also met Julio Matheu Junior, now in the U. S, army and married to a Korean.

Eduardo's parents are now in Europe. His brother Julio runs INFASA. Brother Roberto is a manufacturing representative and a businessman. Pablo works as a manager and advisor for one of the largest cotton producers in Central America.

We walked to the village or "aldea" traversing part of the area and saw the Indian girls coming to get water from a small spring where there is a big "pila." Houses in the village are of concrete block with tin roofs. The latter replace all over Guatemala the heavy adobe tile that crashed down on its inhabitants a year earlier literally killing thousands of "Guatemaltecos."

The ceremony was a bit out of the ordinary for us: there was a marimba band and high-flown speechifying. It was interesting to hear the engineer in charge and the army colonel. But the show was stolen by the Tecpán "cofrades" (elders) who walked in "en masse" in the middle of the speeches. They wore felt hats, white shirts, no tie, and a dark jacket with a brown and white checked sash about the waist. The speeches were again interrupted by fireworks and marimba songs. A pretty Indian girl in a beautiful "huipil" presented a banner and gift of a weaving to the Colonel.

It was interesting to watch all the Indians gathered, especially the elders, and the Mayor Martín Chuy.

Roland Bunch, the author of the "Highlands Maya" book, Chuck Atlee of the International Development Agency and a Quaker girl joined us for lunch.

What followed was a nice ride to the lake, to the beach, then to dinner, a nice meal on main street Panajachel.

On the ride back to the house Mark suddenly was struck with bad stomach trouble and spent a very bad night. "I thought I would die." There were bad stomach cramps most of the night. As I redo these notes, I am wondering if I should ever return to Guatemala with my gringo stomach! But there was a good side of that night: I awoke at one moment to see the lake bathed in a sinking moon in the west. Gorgeous!

We woke up early for a walk up into the fields from the lake. At that time of day the lake is tranquil. There were lots of birds in the bushes and Santa Catarina Indians on the way to Panajachel. Men were up in the fields planting onions and watering. You could see the trails winding way up the mountain. These were tiny garden plots, but beautiful.

The Santa Catarina women wear a bright red "huipil," a blue "corte" or skirt with a red stripe, and a red cloth on the head. The men are in straw, cowboy-style hats, dye-tied striped shirts and "incredible' woven pants, broad to just below the knee. Birds and all are woven into the fabric.

There were men in dugout canoes, "cayucos," on the lake.

We went into Panajachel for mass, and it was beautiful in its simplicity. There was a tiny organ and two song leaders. It was mainly Indians from Sololá (with "rodillera, pantalones, y chumpas blancas de murciélago"). Many of the women were with babies. The Santa Catarina women had necklaces bright gold or silver in color, colored beads and bright ribbons in their hair. They all seemed very beautiful.

After mass and the return to the cabin, Keah and I did a "paseo" to Santa Catarina. We stopped at very poor, mud houses on the way, in the middle of a coffee grove (and not their coffee by the way). The Indian ladies were poor looking except for the weaving and clothing.

We then walked down to the beach by the lake, a beautiful scene. Men were either resting or working on the "cayucos," heating pine pitch to apply to cracks between the wood. Women, all in native costume, were washing clothes or their hair or their children. One sees many small garden plots with very healthy looking vegetables along the bank.

We walked up to the church and noted once more the statue of the Virgin, she dressed completely in Indian garb.

We walked back to the house, down to the beach with the Matheus and enjoyed the sun, and watching Eduardo snorkel and the Indians fish. I snorkeled a bit myself; but the water was murky and cool with sudden cold currents. Lake Atitlán has dropped several meters since the earthquake; no one knows exactly why.

We had a nice lunch, a nap and then the drive back to the city with rain and fog. Ugh!

So this was a great visit with the Matheus and we got along well. Harry is neat. Keah enjoyed it once again and is doing fine, now in the 6th month now of the pregnancy.

Trip to the Verapaces, 1977

In 1977 after the summer school was concluded, all the paperwork done and the goodbyes made, Keah and I decided to do something new in Guatemala—a tourist trip to the Verapaces in northeast Guatemala. Our Guide was Federico Von Quenov. He studies tourism and hotel management at the Universidad Javier Landívar in Guatemala. He was born and raised on a "finca" hear Cobán and is multi-lingual. His co-guide and driver friend was Francisco an exchange student from Boston.

Other travelers were Dóna Marga, a Jewish lady living in Guatemala since 1939 and the Schmidts, he a professor at the German College and his wife.

We left Guatemala City on a Saturday, on the road that heads to the Atlantic coast and passed by the temporary bridge since the earthquake and then proceeded up to an arid area near El Progreso.

Then we began to climb, leaving the cactus country and entering into the pines. There was a rest stop at the "Finca de los Leones" of some Germans in the region. Then we drove through a very mountainous zone with very green valleys where there is a green marble deposit and country huts with straw roofs. All seemed poor and the climate was very humid.

Then we came to an overlook of the beginnings of the Valley of Baja Verapaz. There were pine trees in this large valley about 25 kilometers long. The valley is irrigated by "acequias." In former days the Dominican Friars raised grapes and made a very fine wine here, "a rival to the wines of Peru." But in 1870 the anti-clerical president Barrios expropriated the lands from the church. Today the current owners raise corn, sugar cane and make "aguardiente."

The Town of San Jerónimo, Baja Vera Paz.

The White Façade of a Country Church

It is at the head of the valley; the town on the other end is San Miguel Chicá. And the better known town of Rabinal is in the vicinity. We saw the church dating from 1544, simple but with fine altars with some gold. The images are all guarded (kept) in a poor, humid room in the government building on the plaza. The church is white, simple and with crosses of carved wood. There is a central fountain in the plaza where pilgrims or "peregrinos" arrived from Cobán in Alta Vera Paz on their way to Guatemala City. The convent to the side, now in ruins, at one time had 50 friars. The religious travelers, pilgrims, lodged in the convent.

In the plaza is a very large Ceiba tree. The plaza was originally built by the Catholic friars to hold a large cross and the atrium was for the purpose of "Christianizing" the Indians who at first were afraid to enter the church proper.

Outside of San Jerónimo there were many small lakes which were fish hatcheries.

Some 10 kilometers to the west is Salamá, Baja Vera Paz. We passed over the Rio de la Libertad, an important site in the independence of Guatemala. The cathedral in Salamá was reconstructed the first time in 1814 (after earthquakes). In it is a mixture of baroque altars with neo-classic, the latter unusual. Some of the baroque altars with gold gilt had been painted the color of "caoba." The church was first built in the 1540s.

Tactic, Alta Vera Paz

The road now was the prettiest thus far on the trip; we climbed first from the Valley of Baja Vera Paz on the road to Cobán. The road traversed green pastures, pine trees, etc. In one part, a stretch of 4-10 kilometers, there is very dense forest, humid, with many waterfalls. It was a "detour" because they believe there are still Quetzales there. We did not see any.

Then we passed through "The Switzerland of Guatemala." There were long valleys, green and beautiful with lots of cattle, and small, clear streams. There were tall mountains with the clouds low on them; it all seemed similar to the mountains near us in Colorado and green like the Andes we saw in Colombia.

Elderly Maya Lady with Regional "Huipil"

In a small town along the way we had a pleasant conversation with an Indigenous family in the town of Kejchi. We bought 1/3 of a huipil for $8.50; all we could afford or wanted to spend at the time.

The Road to San Cristóbal de la Alta Verapaz

For several kilometers the pavement was small rocks. The area was humid, with bananas, sugar cane, corn and dense underbrush. One had the feeling we were deep in the interior of Guatemala, the "boonies" as it were.

The town was poor with clay streets and Indians with simple "huipiles," not the highly embroidered ones we were used to seeing. All the ladies had their hair in braids, like Anita, one of the maids in "el Hogar del Turista."

Most impressive was the church and the plaza. We were fortunate to catch a procession of the members of the religious brotherhood or "cofradía" carrying all the saints. They use the term: "Llevarlos de paseo" ("Taking the saints for a walk).

The guide says: In Guatemala in each Indigenous town there are several "barrios." Each part of town has its own patron saint. The members of the brotherhood "take care of" and are in charge of the saints' images and they organize the feast day for each. Each person in that part of town contributes food for the fiesta. Each member of the "cofradía" has a tall, ornate, silver rod as a symbol of his role in the brotherhood.

Members of the "Cofradía"

Procession of the "Saints"

The Procession outide the Church

So in this town we saw the members of the brotherhood, each dressed in black, each with the silver staff or rod with three small bells. A rosary was being said inside the church; the brotherhood sat to one side, the Indian ladies on the other, all dressed in feast day clothes and holding candles. Pum! All of a sudden the procession was leaving the church with three statues, all very Indian in appearance. A man with a drum walked in front, then Indian ladies with tall candles. Then came the statues. The idea is that the brotherhood takes three images or statues to the church to "hear mass" or "oír misa." They then carry them back to the "cofradía" quarters, and then bring three more to "oír misa" on Sunday. I surmise it all gets a bit busy.

The plaza was pretty and was full of natives in town for the festival. The boys and men had straw hats. There were few "ladinos" or whites.

On the Road to Santa Cruz, Alta Verapaz

We passed by a lake with a certain duck found only in that region. The locals fish for bass with a harpoon, and the catch was good.

The town of Santa Cruz is extremely poor with Indians all about. We arrived at about dusk. The church is old with gilt altars and a reddish color (like the San Francisco in Bogotá).

The market seemed to have many more persons dressed in the "ladino" or white man's style. There were loud speakers and marimba music.

Cobán, Alta Verapaz

After all the hoopla, Cobán being a much larger and important place, the town did not impress us much. In spite of being the "capital" of the province, it is very poor in appearance. We stayed in the "Hotel Central," poor and with no hot water. The good hotels were already full, the Oxib Pek and La Posada, full because of Indigenous congresses. The Sunday morning breakfast was indeed "very Guatemalteco" with fried eggs, black beans, cheese and sweet rolls. While in Cobán we saw and climbed the Cerro del Calvario. It dates from 1543 and the last indigenous chief in the region. Then we saw the Convento de Fray Bartolomé de las Casas and the Catedral de Cobán. The original name of Cobán is "Chimoja," a Kejchi name.

The Road to San Juan Chamelco

We traveled on a road paved with rocks, very narrow and hilly, passing by small "ranchos" of the natives: there was generally a "milpa" with a mud hut by its side with a thatch roof. All seemed very poor. The soil did not seem so rich and was very rocky.

We passed by many natives that morning, some already drunk, headed for the festival day of San Juan Chamelco. Many wore the "sombreros de tres picos" with small mirrors on them for the "Baile de los Moros."

The Native Ladies and Their Babies Awaiting Baptism

In San Juan the façade of the church was impressive, poor but colorful: with lions and angels painted on it. Inside it was dark and empty. But an interesting scene ensued: there were many indigenous ladies, some nine in all, all with babies to be baptized, all the mothers dressed in "Huipil, falda y collares."

Outside in the plaza there was a small fair with miniature Ferris wheels and carnival games to take the Indians' money: a coin toss, revolving roulette with prizes, Viewmasters, and food stands with "huaro" or sugar cane fire water.

After this village we wound our way back down the country roads to Guatemala City.

Impressions of the Trip

The countryside in the Verapaces was at times beautiful with forests and valleys. The towns were extremely poor, but there is something "enchanting" about their plazas, always with a large La Ceiba Tree. The churches were pretty, but were now almost all empty due to robbery and the significant damage from the last earthquake. There was an almost complete lack of saints' images or paintings (these can be found in the "cofradia" buildings). The altars were pretty however.

The most striking was the "picturesqueness" of the Indians, the way the ladies carry themselves and walk, the ornate woven clothing (when they wear it rather than "ladino" modern dress) and the religious customs we saw.

In the end, I would recommend the trip for anyone interested in the history of Verapaces and especially in small indigenous churches. But in comparison to the west (Antigua, Atitlán, or Chichicastenango) it is poor, and in spite of the amount of native clothing we saw, it seemed less interesting than the region of Sacatepéquez and the lake.

GUATEMALA SADLY COMES TO AN END

This completes my notes for the summer of 1977. Shortly after the Verapaces trip Keah and I flew home to Phoenix, then drove to Colorado where we stayed at the small house of good friends Jerry and Kassy Rebensdorf in Ouray. Keah by now was "very pregnant indeed." We returned home late that August and then in September to await the baby, little Kathleen who arrived on September 29, 1977. Times would change as the family grew, and I no longer had any contact with the ASU Guatemala Summer School, but it was indeed an important chapter in the growing interest in things Maya.

There will be a hiatus in travel to Meso-America, but serious study and teaching about Guatemala and Mexico and their respective Pre-Colombian cultures would continue at ASU, really until my retirement in 2002. But a golden opportunity was presented to us in 1998 when we would travel again, surely to some previously visited sites, but also to many of the places I had always dreamed about. Those travels involve Mexico and are narrated with many photo illustrations in Volume II—Mexico.

APPENDICES

In the following pages I include some of the "nitty-gritty" of years of study and compiling sources of study of Guatemala, Mexico, the quest for knowledge of the Pre-Colombian Civilization and some modern developments as well. This material all appeared in the syllabi for the upper division class for Spanish Majors at Arizona State University, SPA 472, Spanish American Civilization, as well as the "Get Away" Program at Fort Lewis College in Durango years later, and in Colorado during retirement, most recently in adult culture courses in English at the Pine River Public Library in Bayfield, Colorado, where I have had the privilege of sharing knowledge, tourism and fun with folks in retirement. It is most important to understand that these are DIFFERENT sources for the SAME topics; they may both repeat and complement each other. But each has concepts and facts that may not be repeated in other sources. The reader should peruse them and simply take from them what is of interest. Each item can be used as a point of departure to be searched on the internet. What will be revealed is the complexity of the topics.

1. Suggested Readings: General Books on Latin America
2. A List of Topics and Questions on Pre-Colombian Civilization from the Course SPA 472 Spanish-American Civilization at Arizona State University
3. Suggested Readings on Pre-Columbian Cultures from National Geographic Magazine
4. The Professor's Notes from "Mundo Maya."
5. The Professor's Notes from Documentary Films on the Mayas

1. SUGGESTED READINGS. GENERAL BOOKS: LATIN AMERICAN CIVILIZATION

Continente (el) de Siete Colores. Germán Arciniegas

Cultural (A) History of Spanish America, from the Conquest to Independence. Mariano Picón-Salas

History and Conquest of Mexico and Peru. Prescott

History of Latin American Civilization. Hanke

Incidents of Travel in Central America, Chiapas and Yucatan. John Stephens. Illustrations by Catherwood. 2 volumes

Latin America: an Historical Survey. Bannon

Latin America the Development of Its Civilization. Bailey

Latin American Civilization. Benjamin Keen. Vol. 1, 1974

Linda Schele. Writings on the Maya and the Glyphs

David Stuart. Writings on the Maya and the Glyphs

Many Mexicos. Lesley Bird Simpson

Modern Culture of Latin America. Jean Franco

Rise and Fall of Mayan Civilization. John E. Thompson

2. A LIST OF TOPICS FOR PRE-COLUMBIAN LATIN AMERICA FROM THE COURSE ON LATIN AMERICAN CIVILIZATION AT ARIZONA STATE UNIVERSITY—SPA 472

This list of topics and names was presented in lectures, slide lectures and readings for the course "Spanish American Civilization SPA 472." For the purposes of this book, each topic is presented to whet the reader's curiosity. One can "Google" each and learn much more than space permits in this volume. As the reader peruses the long list however, he/she will recognize some topics touched upon in our narration.

I.   Introduction to Latin American Civilization

1.   The question and differences between culture and civilization (according to anthropology)
2.   Elements of a civilization
3.   The three major river systems of Latin America
4.   La pampa
5.   The Andes—a natural barrier
6.   The Amazon
7.   The concept of monoculture
8.   Origen of the American native: the Behring Strait
9.   The concept of "mestizaje" or the mixture of races
10. The concept of "syncretism" or the mixture of religions
11. "El Teocintle," ancestor to corn (maize), a key to civilization?
12. Primitive early cultures: Tiajuanaku (Alto Peru) and Teotihuacán (Central Mexico)

II. Pre-Columbian Meso-America

1.   The Olmecs. The "Mother" or Proto-culture, characteristics
2.   Teotihuacán, the first great city, pyramids, Temple and Legend of Quetzalcóatl
3.   The Mayas, the "Greeks" of America. Why?
4.   The Mayan codices: the glyphs. Where? Themes?
5.   The "Popol Vuh," a post-conquest text. The Creation Story. Written in Mayan language with Roman letters.
6.   Writing on the stelae ("estelas"). What is it like? Its purpose? Where? Variations?
7.   The stelae of Tikal, analogy with the "Renaissance"
8.   The stelae of Copán, analogy of the "Baroque"
9.   Mayan painting: the frescos of Bonampak (and their influence on Diego Rivera)
10. Stephens and Catherwood. "Incidents of Travel in Central America, Chiapas and Yucatan." Stephens the American diplomat; Catherwood the artist.
11. Michael Coe. "The Maya"

12. The "sacbé," the Maya road between different sites, i.e. at Uxmal in the Yucatan

13. The lintel ("dintel"): the wooden carved beam above doorways of Mayan temples, carved with figures and glyphs in the same style as the stelae (in stone)

14. Tikal: the main urban center of the early classic period in Guatemala and the influence of Teotihuacán at the site

15. The "katun" maya: a period of twenty years, often marking the new construction of temples and other edifices

16. The Maya religion: polytheistic, related to the forces of nature and mother earth. It was related to the study of the stars, star and planet movement and the development of mathematics (the long count). There was a close relationship to agriculture as well, i.e. sun, rain and soil.

17. Late classic Maya sites in the Yucatán: Uxmal and Chichén-Itzá (the latter a Maya-Toltec hybrid)

18. Kukulcán: God of the Plumed Serpent in the Yucatan; the same god as Quetzalcóatl of the Toltecs in Tula, near the Valley of Mexico

19. The Maya arch ("la media bóveda"): not a true, rounded arch, it was supported by a capstone which determined the size and shape of temples and interior rooms.

20. Economic base for the Maya: agriculture of maize, squash, beans and chile. This evolved to the "milpa" in Central America. The masses or "pueblo" lived in the countryside and were responsible for the labor of agriculture.

21. Government and dynasties in the larger classic centers, hereditary rule, a family of nobility who also ruled in priesthood and the military. The classes: nobility/ warriors/ priests/artisans/ rural commoners/ slaves.

22. Theories for the end of the Classic Age of the Maya: drought, soil depletion, and more recently, warfare.

III. The Toltecs

1. Their supposed origin was near Cuernavaca in Mexico.

2. The first known leader or chief was Mixcóatl; at his death Quetzalcóatl.

3. Founding and the grandeur of Tula

4. Man or legend? Quetzalcóatl, the "Feathered Serpent." He supposedly had the attributes of the good and was the giver of corn to the Indigenous peoples.

5. The legend at Tula: Quetzalcóatl is challenged to battle by Tezcatlipoca, god of the night. Tezcatlipoca succeeds in getting Quetzalcóatl drunk, convinces him he has had relations with his own sister, and he must face shame and banishment. There are three versions of the legend form:

   a. He goes to the East and is converted into Venus, the morning star.

b. He migrates with his people to the East, South and eventually to the Yucatán and Chichén-Itzá.

c. He disappears but promises to return one day and restore the former glory to his people, thus providing a later connection to the Aztecs, Moctezuma and the arrival of Cortés.

6. Migration of the Toltec people.

a. One part is believed to migrate to the Valley of Mexico, circa 950 A.D., becoming dominant in the Valley prior to the arrival of the Aztecs.

b. Another part migrated to the East, South and eventually to the Yucatán and to Chichén-Itzá where they join the descendants of the Itzáes to form a hybrid late classic Maya and Toltec civilization.

IV. The Aztecs

1. Their mythical origin was in Aztlán (Place of the Herons). Perhaps in NW New Mexico.
2. Waves of migration of the nomadic peoples called the Chichimecas were probably one and the same as early Aztecs. They moved eventually to central Mexico and Lake Texcoco.
3. The Aztecs were originally nomads, of a poor but violent culture.
4. They, like the Romans, were excellent at absorbing the culture of the peoples they came in contact with and/or conquered, i.e. first the remains of the Toltecs near Tula and later the Toltecs and other peoples in the Valley of Mexico.
5. The Aztecs arrive at Lake Texcoco around 1300 A.D.
6. They survive as mercenaries for other groups, live in poverty, are mistrusted and looked down upon as barbarians by the Toltecs and others. But by virtue of intrigue and warlike demeanor they soon dominated other peoples.
7. The Legend of the Eagle and the Serpent. The legend was given by their god Huitzilopochtli during the migration: they were to establish their land upon seeing and eagle devouring a serpent while perched on a cactus. They had this vision at Lake Texcoco and then established what would become Tenochtitlán (and later Mexico City) in 1325.
8. "Las chinampas." These were the so-called "floating gardens" and were the basis of Aztec agriculture on the lake.
9. William Prescott. "The Conquest of Mexico (and Peru)." 2 volumes
10. Bernal Díaz del Castillo. "La Verdadera Historia de la Conquista de Nueva España." The story of the Spaniards' conquest of Mexico as told by one of his soldiers.
11. Later on came Fray Bartolomé de las Casas and his "Breve Historia de Destrucción de Indias." The defense of the native peoples and the violence of the Spaniards during and

after the conquest. De las Casas would become bishop of San Cristóbal de las Casas and later instrumental in the founding of cities in the Alta Verapaces in Guatemala.

12. The Aztec legend of Huitzilopochtli (god of war, the sun with the symbol of the hummingbird "chupando" or sucking nectar from the flower, symbol of the human heart). The legend tells of the intrigue by his sister, Coyolxauqui, goddess of the moon, and her allies, the stars, in a plot to kill her own mother, Coatlicue. Huitzilopochtli discovers the plot and defeats Coyolxauqui and the stars, supposedly cutting her into pieces. Thus the sun rises each day (conquering the forces of night), but it must be nourished by sacrificial blood ("chauchihuatl"). Scholars believe that this is the true basis for Aztec human sacrifice.

13. The War of the Flowers ("La Guerra Florida"). This is the ritualistic war between the Aztecs and other tribes of the Valley of Mexico; it was done via a pact between them and its purpose was to obtain sacrificial victims for the Aztecs.

14. Nezahuacóyotl. He was the king of Texcoco, a philosopher and poet and adviser to the Aztecs.

15. Fray Bernardo Sahuagún. He did an amazing series of ethnographic studies on the Aztecs after the conquest, no less than 12 volumes.

16. "El Codex Mendoza." This is the principal post-conquest document that is the basis for learning about the Aztecs. It was ordered to be done by the Spanish Viceroy Mendoza circa 1540. It is pictographic with notes in Spanish. Together with Sahuagún's work, it is the basis for later scholarship on the Aztecs.

17. The Great Temple. "El Templo Mayor." Circa 1487. The temple represents the epitome of Aztec power and worship-sacrifice. It is really two temples in one: on one side the temple of Huitzilopochtli, the other dedicated to Tlaloc the Rain God. Quetzalcóatl was adopted by the Aztecs from the Toltecs, and his temple is tall and cylindrical and is located in the same plaza. There are estimates that the inauguration of the Templo Mayor involved 70,000 victims! The stench of flesh and blood disgusted the Spanish when they arrived in Tenochtitlán.

18. Los Pochteca. These refer to the Aztec merchant class; they were used as merchants but also diplomats and perhaps spies. They were essential to the expansion of Aztec dominion.

19. Moctezuma I, Moctezuma II, Cuautémoc: major Aztec leaders.

20. Los "Mixitli." This is an alternative name for the Aztecs, thus the word "Mexico" and "Mexicans."

21. "La Gran Tenochtitlán." The Great Tenochtitlán, was the original Aztec capital and would become Mexico City, D. F. One can see a description of the same by the conqueror Hernán Cortés in his "Cartas de Relación," (letters to the King, a sort of report of the conquest) and Bernal Díaz's "True Conquest of New Spain." It was the greatest center of the the Americas, pre-conquest times, with commerce, religion, government and thought to be a fantastic kingdom like those in the Books of Chivalry read by the Spaniards of the time.

22. Náhua. The Aztec "lingua franca." Quechua was the same in Peru for the Incas.
23. Aztec Fatalism: they believed they were living in the fifth phase of the world, a world already destroyed four times. Human sacrifice and blood sacrifice to appease and soften the ways of the gods to not destroy the earth thus became widespread. They had fear of the end and also had the belief of the coming of Quetzalcóatl, thus Moctezuma's fatal hesitation and wonder at the blond Spaniard Cortés, or so it is written.

V.   Other Pre-Colombian civilizations and cultures

1.   Peru and the Incas
2.   Colombia and the Chibchas
3.   Chile and the Araucanos (see the Spanish American Epic Poem, "La Araucana")
4.   Los Caribes of Venezuela and the Caribbean Islands
5.   Los Tupi-Guaraníes, hunters and gatherers of Brazil.

3. SUGGESTED READINGS ON MESOAMERICAN TOPICS. "NATIONAL GEOGRAPHIC"

(* = Complete Issue)

"Bonampak." February, 1995
"El Mirador." September, 1987
"Following Cortés." October, 1984
"Jade." September,1987
"La Ruta Maya." October, 1989 *
"Maya Artistry." September, 1991
"Maya. Children of Time, Riddle of Glyphs, Tikal." 1975 *
"Mural Masterpieces of Ancient Cacaxtla." September, 1992
"New Light on the Olmec." November, 1993
"Royal Crypts of Copán." December, 1997
"The Golden Grain Corn." June, 1993
"The Oldest Maya." July, 1982.
"Timeless Teotihuacán." December, 1995
"Aztecs—Tenochtitlán, the Great Temple"." December, 1980

Special Series: National Geographic Hardbound Books
"The Aztecs"
"The Incas"
"The Mayas"

4. NOTES AND A SUMMARY OF "MUNDO MAYA"—GUIDE AND INFORMATION FOR THE "RUTA MAYA"

The following pages are the author's notes from a reading of "Mundo Maya." As such they are of course just that, notes! The reader should consider them simply as a brief outline of the book and "Google" any topics of interest. Yet they do have much basic information that has not been touched upon in the main text of this book.

I. HISTORY OF DISCOVERY OF THE MAYA WORLD

1502.   The first contact. One of Columbus' trips landed on the Isle of Guanaja and there was an exchange of objects with natives.

1503.   Hernán de Córdoba reached Isla Mujeres off the Coast of Yucatán.
Then Juan de Grijalva was there and was the first to hear of the Aztecs.
1519. Cortés and 19 ships arrive at today's Vera Cruz, east coast of Mexico.

It will take 200 years to finally subject Yucatan to Spanish/Mexican rule. The Pre-Columbian ruins were largely ignored by the Spanish conquistadores.

Bishop Diego de Landa fought and defeated the Mayas in 1535. He then became the first bishop of Yucatan and wrote "Relación de las Cosas de Yucatán," a work discovered in 1864.

Juan Galindo who had been a bishop in Ireland was in Guatemala in 1827 and was named governor of the Petén Region. He discovered the Copán ruins in 1834 and did maps.

Jean F. Waldeck. 1766-1875. He arrived in Palenque in 1832 at the age of 66. He drew images of the ruins and illustrated the Del Río Book. He believed the European Civilizations were superior and had somehow aided in the forming of New World cultures.

John Stephens 1805-1853. It was he who brought a scientific approach to studies. He determined that the Maya and other cultures were independent of the Old World. Stephens met Catherwood, a British architect, in 1836. Catherwood would be famous for the lithographs of "Incidents of Travel in Central America, Chiapas and Yucatan." Their books opened the Maya world to the general reading public. First trip: Copán, Quiriguá, Toniná and Palenque.

Desiré Charnay. He was the first to photograph the ruins in 1859; they appeared in his book in 1863.

Alfred Maudslay. He made good use of documents and a better photographic technique. He would do four volumes on Maya archeology. 1889-1902.

Teobert Maler. German. He completed Maudslay's work, especially the photography.

(A photographic "aside": Frederick Catherwood used the "clear camera" to get clear pictures from which he made the drawings.)

First Excavations

The first ones in Copán were between 1891-1895 by the Peabody Museum of Harvard.

1914-1958.   The Carnegie Institute of Washington, D.C. in the lead did Chichén and Copán, Kaminaljuyu in the highlands of Guatemala and Uaxactún. These efforts established the thesis and rule: there were three periods of Maya Civilization—Pre-Classic, Classic, and Post-Classic.

1956-1970.   The Tikal Project by the University of Pennsylvania

New Discoveries

In the 1970s the Bonampak paintings were discovered and are important for concepts of war, torture, human sacrifice and auto-sacrifice among the Maya.

1958.   Emblem glyphs are deciphered by Merlin; he discovered that the glyphs were not just number and calendar glyphs, but history. Latest discoveries show the relationship between the Olmecs and the old Maya at El Mirador.

1970s. RussianTatiana Proskouriakoff did extensive work at deciphering the glyphs. It was discovered at Piedras Negras that there was a 60 year maximum difference between constructions of stelae. She figured out that the stelae really depicted the life and lifespan of a given monarch or sovereign. The first date was king's birth, the second his access to throne, and the last was death. So, the inscriptions were not just measures of time or religion.

Note: In 1864 a certain Padre Brasseur who studied the Madrid Codex, monuments in Yucatan and the Landa book sees that all were describing calendar, day and month names and respective glyphs. He came to understand that all represented one writing system with local variants, different from the "signs" of Aztec Codices. Before 1950, all thought that the Mayan language seen in the glyphs was morphemic (syntactic) or words (logographic). Now we know it was also syllabic. The latter work of Linda Schele and David Stuart are both extremely important.

II. MAYA WORLD FROM 1250 TO THE PRESENT

1. The Post Classic 1250-1325. The Mayapan League exists until 1450 at places like Xel-Ha, Tulum, and Cozumel.

    In the high country of Guatemala at the same time there are local capitals:

Mixco Viejo: the Pokomanes
Zaculeu: the Mames
Iximché the Cakchiqueles
Utatlán: the Quichés
At the end of the 15ᵗʰ century the Cakchiqueles were the dominant group.

2. The Conquest

The Spaniard Córdoba appeared off the coast of Yucatán, at Isla Mujeres.

1517:   Then Juan de Grijalva landed on the Peninsula of Yucatán.
1519:   Hernán Cortés took one year to conquer Mexico and the Aztecs.
1523:   Pedro de Alvarado, a lieutenant under Cortés in Mexico, continues on to Guatemala via the Pacific Coast. He eventually conquers the Quiché and their chief Tucun Uman at Utatlán and then the rest at Iximché. His brother defeats the Tzutuiles at Atitlán. Pedro de Alvarado then founds Santiago de los Caballeros in Ciudad Vieja or Almolonga which is destroyed and later rebuilt at Antigua.

In the North in southern Mexico there is resistance to the Spaniards to the point of mass suicide against Luis Marín and Diego de Mazariegos who founds Villa Real in 1524 which later becomes San Cristóbal de las Casas. Pedro de Alvarado had founded Comitán on his way to Guatemala. He and Mazariegos simply divided the lands between them.

3. The Colony

Fray Bartolome' de las Casas and the Dominicans established missions in the highlands of Guatemala in the Verapaces. Much of N. Guatemala and the Yucatan were not conquered right away.

Cortés saw the area for the first time in 1525 on his way to Honduras.

There was Lacandón resistence in Chiapas. In fact, the Mayas were not totally conquered for 200 years.

1542:   the Capitanía of Guatemala was established.
1562:   Guatemala and Yucatan became part of the Viceroyalty of Nueva España.
1567:   The Audiencia de Guatemala was formed.

4.   The Colonial System.

Indians were considered subjects of the Crown. Slavery of the Indians was prohibited after the debates between Pe. Victoria and Pe. Montesinos against the "conquistadores." As a result the "New Laws of the Indies" were promulgated in 1542, but the principles remained on paper; the Americas were a long way from the laws and justice of Spain.

Fray Bartolomé became the first Bishop of Chiapas.

Bishop Landa in Yucatan held an "Auto da Fé" with torture and killing of the Indians who practiced the old religion after being supposedly converted to Catholicism. It was at this time he burned the "códices". Irony: he also was the person responsible for learning most about the Mayas.

Indians were decimated by diseases, mainly smallpox. No Spaniards were allowed in the Indian villages, only Catholic Monks. But the Indian beliefs were what brought on the "Auto da Fe."

Guatemala and Chiapas had no gold and were far from the influence of pirates along the coasts, so agriculture was maintained after the conquest. But Yucatan was different: the Indians attacked the Spaniards and held out independently in Quintana Roo.

England colonizes Belize and British Honduras by the end of 1790.

All Indians were subject to the "encomienda" (the large amount of land granted to Spanish soldiers and others as a "reward" for their work in the conquest: the "encomendero" controlled the land and the Indians on it) until 1716 and then the "repartimiento" (the labor grants to landholders for their own projects with forced labor by the Indians) until 1789. They were subject to payment of tribute to the crown.

5.   Independence

1812:   the "Grito de Independencia" by Miguel Hidalgo followed by the "Cortes" at Cádiz in 1814.
1821:   Mexican Independence
1823:   Central American Independence from Mexico. Chiapas declared independence from Mexico.

1824: A plebiscite is held; Chiapas is now part of Mexico
1839: the United Provinces of Central America end.

6. Post-Independence

Yucatan declares independence from Mexico in 1841.
The Caste Wars threaten whites.
Yucatan is incorporated into Mexico in 1848.

7. Chiapas

It is a mess, conservatives versus liberals, landholders versus Indians up to the present days. 1994: Zapatista Revolution under Comandante Marcos.

8. Guatemala

It becomes a nation in 1839 with liberal government in the first years.

There is a turn to conservative government and dictatorship under the dictator Carrera from 1844-1865.

Liberal government follows under Barrios.

The Twentieth century:

US economic interests rule. General Úbico rules until 1944, then Arévalo.

1954: General Árbens and an agrarian reform is followed by a "golpe de estado" with US backed General Castillo Armas. Many reforms were rescinded and land was given back to companies. Repression followed.
1963: The founding of FAR, revolutionary group on the left, violence, murders, terrorism. But there is right wing death squad counter reaction. Indians flee to Mexico and US in the 1980s. 1985: the violence lessens and a return to "normal," but the damage is done.

III. MAYA HIEROGLYPHIC WRITING

Over 800 glyphs have been counted. Some express concepts, others are syllabic. Manuscripts were called "códices". Only 3 exist now, in libraries in Madrid, Paris and Dresden. They were originally long sheets of bark paper, pleated, covered with lime and painted. The Dresden codex: prophecy and astronomy. The Madrid codex: horoscopes, almanacs.

The text is in rows and columns. It is read from left to right or top to bottom by pairs of columns.

An example: An account of an offering

First glyph is verb; it sets the action to make an offering.
The second glyph is the object: the offering itself.
The third glyph: it names the personage making the offering.
Fourth: This is the resulting prophecy.

You cannot use Maya glyphs for Roman alphabet because the glyphs are syllabic and not letters.

IV. MAYA CALCULATIONS AND CALENDARS

Years are counted according to the number of days since the original year of 3114 B.C. in the Maya long count (the year of the "new" generation of mankind when the gods placed the three hearthstones).

Day: "kin"
Month (20 days) "uinal"
Year of 360 days: "tun"
Period of 20 tun: "katun"
Period of 20 katun (400 years): "biktun"

The Mayas used position arithmetic and the calendar:

The prophecy and ritual cycle: 260 days, the "tzolkin"
The solar year of 365 days: the "haab"
The long count: 5.200 tun X 360 days

Computation allowed them to write HISTORY, but also to predict the future, this due to a cyclical conception of chronological units (cycles which repeat themselves). This is seen in their inscriptions.

Bishop Landa depicted the "katun" cycle in circle form, showing 13 katun (20 years each).

The short count is an event (a given date) related to the end of a specific "katun" (20 years).

Between two fixed "katuns" were 260 "tun" (260 X 360 days).

There was a cycle of 52 years: you can abbreviate the long count by indicating the date of the "tzolkin" (260 days) and the date of the "haab" (365 days). The combination of the positions of these two cycles could not repeat more than once every 52 years.

Astronomic observations of eclipses were noted in the Dresden Codex using the long count system.

Numbers:

They are read not left to right (ex. Our year of 1995) but bottom to top with a base of 20 instead of decimal system.

Bottom level: the units 0-19
Next up: the units of 20
Next up: the units of 400
Next up: the units of 160,000

Example: the year 1995

. . . (4 X 400) = 1600

. . .
Bar
Bar (19 X 20 = 380)
Bar

Bar
Bar (15)
Bar

For a total of 1995

There was a second calculation system by the use of glyphs which symbolized the numbers and periods of certain initial series which precede an inscription or indicate the time passed since the initial first day of the Maya long count.

Ex. A date from Stela E of Quiriguá. There are different glyphs at different sites.

Note: if all the above seems confusing, I am told that it is not confusing to the mathematicians. But much of it is truly "Greek" to me.

V. HUMAN SACRIFICE AND SELF-SACRIFICE AMONG THE MAYAS

There was far less sacrifice than with Aztecs or Toltecs, but ritual human sacrifice was practiced and was an element of Maya religion from the very beginnings.

Sacrifice of others or oneself had equal value—payment to the natural and supernatural powers if you wanted something from them: rain, good crops, victory in battle, or smooth passage of time through the universe.

Self-sacrifice: offering of one's own blood obtained at the end of suffering. They used manta ray stingers, knives or other sharp objects to extract the blood. Ex. A cord with spines passed through the tongue of the person sacrificing his/ her blood.

Best example of the cord with spines: a stela with low-relief from Yaxchilán

Sacrifice of others: tearing out the heart of a victim, especially after 1000 AD at Chichén; this was seen on the pectoral gold disks retrieved from the "cenote" or well at Chichén. Note that this was due to the Central Mexican influence from Toltecs.

Example: the "tzompantli" (skull rack) monument at Chichén which is very similar to the one at Tenochtitlán by Aztecs.

Probably all the Mayas were expected to give blood sacrifice at some time, but religious and political leaders, especially the king or his wife were expected to do this more often. The concept was: the greater the pain, the greater the value of the sacrifice. Ex. Blood from penis by knife, ex. Blood from the tongue via cord with spines.

(For all this see our notes to the film "Blood of Kings: the Maya").

Sacrificial scenes were rarely depicted on the monuments, but the instruments of sacrifice which were associated with images of the nocturnal sun (the jaguar) are common.

Sacrifices were often to the sun to give it the strength to be reborn each day.
Or to the earth for fecundity.

Types of sacrifice of others:

Decapitation or tearing out of heart or both. The heart was destined to the sun and the blood flow from decapitation for the thirst of the land.

VI. MAYA CERAMICS

Objects included whistles, incense burners, figures of dancers or warriors. The Mayas burned copal in the incense burners; the smoke was the way to communicate with the deceased ancestors, with the nightly sun, with mother earth and other natural sources. The smoke carries the prayers or pleas.

Note: The Mayas burned "paper" with the blood drippings from the penis of the King; the smoke communicated the prayers or offerings.

Such incense burners were used from the old Classic to Mayapán.

VII. MAYA COSMOGENY (VIEW OF THE UNIVERSE)—CLASSIC AND POST-CLASSIC MAYA

It depended on whom you rendered cult.

In the pre-classic and classic times, it was to natural forces: the land, earth, death, corn, lightning, etc. in the form of hybrid beings or symbols whose images could change.

In post-classic times, the images no longer changed and each came to take on personality, thus converting itself into a deity, part of an unchanging pantheon.

An example from the early phase is the Cosmic Monster, both celestial and of the underworld at the same time. It was natural-supernatural and life-death at same time. The monster may have two heads, one terrestrial and alive, one of the night sun and not in the flesh. An example of this is seen in of the stelae at Copan: the human figure and the "sun" monster in the front view.

Other examples: creatures associated with fertility, often reptilian symbols or creatures with feline characteristics depicted as solar beings.

Others were spirits of sacrifice, war, or death. The cycle was life to death and death to rebirth.

Primacy of the King: in the monuments the king constituted the center of the universe and the cosmic powers were shown around him, the latter usually represented by monsters or grotesque figures which were more "spirits" than gods. Often the earth or underworld monster (spirit?) would be depicted below the king and an image of heaven or sky above his head.

It is important to note that in the post-classic (Chichén and beyond) there were changes. Stelae were no longer sculpted, thus the king and Maya spirits of natural forces were no longer done.

Instead the carvings were from Mexico and the subjects were warriors, rivals in warfare. There were scenes of war and human sacrifice. Ex. The temple of the jaguars and eagles at Chichén.

Gods were portrayed and mainly Mexican gods: Quetzalcóatl (Kukulcán) and Huitzilopochtli. Plus, the people of these times began to put post-classic names on the images of the old Maya monuments, thus these more recent names are most likely incorrect; the original images were of natural forces or spirits.

Example: the "masks" at Uxmal and old Chichén. Because of the large "nose" they were called "chacs" or rain gods, but were really masks of the "cosmic monster" or "terrestrial monster".

VIII. MAYA ARCHITECTURE

They lacked the wheel, beast of burden and metals. The major goal of their buildings was to impress! The arch gave height so it was emphasized. Traits of their architecture:

1. The sculptured parament
2. Stones joined by mortar
3. The bases: platforms to make a pyramid
4. The Maya arch (4 variations)

It rests on two walls which as they go higher are angled and topped by a horizontal capstone. They were constructed by using an "armazón" or scaffolding of wood. They used a lime kiln to make lime and mortar from limestone which is then burned.

5. Sculpted decoration of walls, in relief
6. Stuccoes: walls, ex. Palenque. The walls were of stucco and then painted.
7. Frescos on walls and arches of interiors. Ex. Bonampak
8. Use of polychrome: blue, red, yellow, white

IX. MAYA TEMPLES

1. They were constructed on top of each other.
2. They used several platforms with a sanctuary or temple on top.
3. Examples: the "temple-pyramid" at Tikal, Palenque or Chichén
4. The Maya "palace". Long rooms on each level, perhaps 2-3-4 levels. ex. Sayil ex. Uxmal
5. Variant: a palace with "false" temples. At Rio Bec in the Yucatan there is a "palace" with three "false" pyramids. The steps cannot be climbed.

X. THE PYRAMID

It was built on terraced platforms. There was a stairway, possibly with carved glyphs on the stones of stairway (Copán, maybe Dos Pilas). At times the glyphs were of defeated enemies which were literally "walked" upon in order to climb the stairs (at Tamarindito). The pyramid may or may not be a tomb (one at Tikal, one at Copán and one at Palenque so far). Many have a roof comb ("cresteria") which at times is taller than the temple itself. It may rest on the back wall of temple, or middle wall or in front (in back at Tikal, in the middle at Palenque and in front in Yucatán). The temple or sanctuary: perhaps in the form of a primitive hut ("choza"). An example is found at the tomb at Palenque.

XI. THE STELAE

They were carved and existed for political and sacred used; they commemorate events generally related to a monarch, but also mythic events.

There is an altar associated with each stela: it exists for sacrifice or an offering related to the dynastic event. Both stelae and altars were placed at the foot of pyramids or temples.

The stela is carved from a single block at the quarry; the finished stone might be rolled on logs and drawn by ropes to the final site. It was raised by gradually building terraces of soil underneath. It was carved on 1, 2, 3, or 4 sides, and generally painted. If a side was smooth, it probably had a stucco finish with text and decorations.

One example: on one side the king might be carved, on two other sides there was text or inscription. The stelae were 1, 2, or 3 meters high; the ones at Quiriguá are the tallest; one is 11 plus meters.

Example: Stela n. 22 at Tikal and accompanying altar showing a sacrificial prisoner.
Example: Zoomorphic altars at Copán: man-animal spirits?

XII. THE MAYA BALL GAME

It was probably more ritual than sport, life forces versus death forces (seen in symbols). At times the outcome was seen as a divine judgment and victims were decapitated, that is, the losers or their representatives.

Each major site had one or more ball courts; the most famous is at Chichén, the most interesting perhaps at Copán.

Chichén: there are vertical walls with benches above and carvings on the sides of the walls.

Copán: the walls are inclined, angled, with parrot markers, open at the end. The markers were perhaps to indicate the end of the playing zone, often were round, carved in stone or stucco.

At the end of the classic period, ball courts had rings on the walls at Uxmal and Chichén (but not at Copán or Tikal which were earlier and were classic sites). In the game held at a place with rings, it was rare to make a "goal", but if one were made, the game ended, the winners obviously the ones who made the "goal."

Players "hit" a heavy rubber ball with hips, elbows and only one side of the body. The ball was passed among players. They wore "protectors" on the waist, some in the form of a U or yoke, on the arm and knee on one side.

An Aside: A type of ball court and ball game was found in New Mexico and Arizona primitive cultures, some estimates place it at 200 sites. Wapaki north of Flagstaff has a reconstructed ball court which is impressive. Rubber balls were found at a few sites. Another question entirely is the contact between Central Mexico, southern Mexico and the U.S. Southwest. Casas Grandes in Chihuahua State may have been important as a major "in between" site.

XIII. MAJOR CLASSIC SITES.

A.   PALENQUE. Its apogee was in the 7th century AC, decline in the 9th.
     First modern explorers: Stephens and Catherwood in 1841.

The Palace: really 15 buildings in the complex, 200 years in the making under 6 kings. Not a residence but a religious center for king and his priest.
First great king: Pacal 615-683 AD

The Cross Grouping. Done by Chan Balam, son of Pacal, 683.

Tallest is the Temple of the Cross, the place of origin of the supernatural world and world of man.
Temple of the Sun: the "nocturnal sun" represented by the jaguar of the subterranean world.
Temple of the Foliated Cross: the rebirth of fertility of the "upper levels" of the earth.

Pryamid of the Inscriptions.

This is a funerary monument to King Pacal. Note that the Mayas were always eager to trade gold to obtain green stones; the Spanish gave them green glass beads! On the walls of the inside temple at the top of the massive exterior stairway there are three panels called "lintels" of carved glyphs, 717 blocks in all, one of the largest of Maya inscriptions. The tomb of Pacal deep in the interior of the pyramid was discovered only in 1952 (some same 1957) by Mexican archeologist Alberto Rus. The stone covering the tomb shows Pacal falling into the jaws of the earth monster. Above him is a mask in fantastic style, not realism, representing the "infra world" with a sacred tree from the four corners of the world. There is a bicephal serpent, that is, two headed, deemed to be an image of heaven. And there is a quetzal at the top: the day sun at its apogee. On the walls: 10 carved figures emerging from the earth, the "counselors of Pacal."

B. YAXCHILÁN.

The site is on the Río Usumacinta, close to Bonampak in Mexico. It is known for excellent interior sculptures. There is a stela or perhaps panel—dintel 26—from 719 AD.
The profiles of personages show the deformed forehead done with a wooden press on Maya babies. The Iconography of Yaxchilán: the images always represent a king or a member of his family. One shows auto-immolation: the famous carving of the Maya woman with a cord with spines through her tongue kneeling before the king. Was this an offering to the king?

Other depictions from Yaxchilán:

Ex. Capture scenes with names of victors and victims
Ex. A basket with ray stingers, pieces of paper with royal blood
Ex. The capture scenes are the most detailed and varied of Maya art.

C. TIKAL

It is located in the lowlands of Northern Guatemala, called the Petén, which comprise one-third of all Guatemalan territory. The region traditionally had closer economic ties to Mexico and Belize than to Guatemala and even had some secession sentiment. Since 1970 there have been 300,000 migrants from the poor highlands to this area along with some government sponsored migration (similar to Brazil's move to the Amazon). This area is second only to Brazil in ecological ruination. The cycle comprises: slash and burn, the planting of beans and corn, crops lessen, cattle are allowed to enter and run. Whatever titles to land the poor peasants had were gradually taken by large landholders and the military. There is general deforestation: one "caoba" tree goes for $7,000 to $10,000 US. Ten million dollars are annually taken out.

The main points of Tikal are:

Pyramids 1, 2, 3, 4, 5
Stelae
North Acropolis
Central Acropolis

A more detailed description is as follows.

The Twin Pryamid Complexes: built each "katun" or twenty years.

North side: a stela and altar
East side; a small pyramid with 4 stairways
West side: the same
South side: a rectangular building with 9 doors
Ex. Group AE4. It was built by King C in 771 to celebrate the end of the 17th "katun." The north side has stela 22. Stela 22 represents King C during rites of celebration at the end of the "katun." Grains or pearls fall from the right hand; the left hand holds a scepter. A supernatural creature appears above his head. Theory: This was to guarantee order for the next twenty years and confronting any doubts as to future.

North Acropolis: 100 X 80 meters. Eight funerary temples built over 300 years.

The Kings of Tikal:

The oldest stela represents a king with an inscription with his name. Name: Jaguar Paw or "Pata de Jaguar." 300-350 A.D. His successor unknown.
Then, "Raised Nose" 379-426 (stela 4)
His son: Stormy Heaven, 426-457 (stela 31, the one in the Museum, the back entirely of glyphs)
Each king is symbolized by a glyph, each has his own.

D. UAXACTUN is 30 k. north of Tikal. A pre-classic, then classic site abandoned in 10th.

E. CEIBAL, late classic period, contemporary of Uaxactun.

Region of the Southeast Maya

F. COPÁN

The fault that separates the North American continental plate from the Central American plate is between Guatemala City and Esquipulas. The 1976 quake split and raised the highway one meter.

The "Valle de Copán." It is known for tobacco (from Cuba) and coffee.

Copan. V-IX centuries AD. It was a rival of Quiriguá, 50 k to the north. The major monuments are:

1. Plaza Mayor (with the stelae)
2. Ball field

3. Patio of the Hieroglyphic stairway
4. Temple 22
5. East patio
6. West Patio

Copán was first described in 1572, then in a letter by Spanish colonial administrator in 1576 to the King of Spain, the letter only discovered in 1860.
Modern discovery: Stephens and Catherwood in 1841

1885 Maudslay and first photos

Highlights of Copán:

The Ball Court.

It is in the form of a capital I, closed at the north end by steps and stelae. It is open at the south end. There are three markers on the sides: three parrot heads, round, perhaps a symbol of "day sun." More ritual than game, it all symbolizes forces of life versus those of death.

The stelae.

Most are "portraits" of the king "standing on one of his great faces." The rest of the stela is inscriptions with glyphs. Usually there is an altar in front of the stela.

The famous square altar (altar Q)

This quadrangular block depicts the 16 kings of Copán and was carved in 776 A.D. It is not the representation of the so-called 16 priest-astronomers and mathematical invention of 0 as previously thought. Copán from about 400 AD to 800 AD had 16 successive kings in the dynasty.

n.b. Stela B. Depicts the ascension to the throne of 18 Rabbit, his head coming out of the jaws of earth monster (thus relating the king to the rising sun).

G. QUIRIGUÁ. Originally depending upon Copán, it was liberated in 737 when Q king defeats 18 Rabbit at Copán. Then it enjoys 100 years at its own apogee. The last date for one of its famous stelae is 810 AD. Quiriguá has the tallest Maya stelae, one of which is 11 meters done in 771. It shows the King standing on a mask of the earth monster (depicted as a jaguar).

WESTERN YUCATAN AND THE PUUC REGION

The center was at Uxmal, but also at old Chichén. This area and style represent a transition between the Classic and Post-Classic eras to approximately 1100 AD. "Old" Chichén was built in the late classic.

Geography: there are no rivers above ground, so water was supplied by excavated wells or "chutuns" and natural wells called "cenotes." The deepest was at Chichén, see the Catherwood sketch.

The Puuc Route: it includes Uxmal, Kabah, Sayil and Labná.

The cultural apogee of this region was from 800-1000 AD. It fell into decline with the arrival of the Toltecs from Central Mexico which ushered in the Post-Classic.

H. UXMAL. No one knows of its exact origins. It has stelae, but none are dated. We do know of a Lord Chac who ruled at the beginning of the 10th century.

First explorer to the region was Waldeck in 1836. Later Stephens and Catherwood. The site was excavated in 1928 and 1938.

Governor's Palace. 1000 meters long, 12 meters wide, 9 meters high.

There are 13 doors and 20 rooms.
There is mosaic decoration on the façade, est. 20,000 sculpted blocks.
The central door: has the image of the King in the center on a throne of two-headed serpents, similar in style that of the Nun's Quadrangle.

The Nun's Quadrangle. 76 X 61 meters.

North side: there is a terrace built on a stairway, two small buildings on either end of stairway.
The façade has 11 doorways: each is a mask with the terrestrial monster above.
There is a large mask of a "pseudo-Tlaloc" and representations of huts or "chozas."
South Side: there are huts and a mask of the earth monster.
West Side: It is more complex in style. There are many super-imposed masks, personages over a "doselete" with warriors in relief, all marked by feathered serpents.

Pryamid of the Magician. There are two temples on top. A King of Uxmal is shown coming out of a serpent's mouth. cf. p. 225.

House of Turtles—symbol of the earth.

I. CHICHÉN—ITZÁ

The old part is originally of the late classic Mayan period of Puuc Architecture. The "new" part is of Putún or Chontal Maya and Toltec.

In the 10th century the Putún Maya (perhaps from Southern Mexico) and Toltecs established a new capital in Chichén-Itzá. Their chief had a Mexican name of Quetzalcóatl (winged serpent) put into Maya as "Kukulcán." This Putún rule lasted 200 years. Tribute was forced upon outlying groups. Chichén later fell into decadence and it was known by the Spaniards at that point. Later, it became a pilgrimage center because of the large "cenote." This was described in writings by Diego de Landa in the 16th century. Stephens and Catherwood arrived in 1841 and did the description and sketches. Then at the end of the 19th Maler and Mauldslay arrived. Then Thompson and the Peabody Expeditions. It was excavated by the Carnegie Institute in 1924.

So the south part (oldest) was Puuc Maya style; the north (new) was Mexican.

The Nun's Annex in the old part. The doorway is an earth monster's mouth. Above: the statue of a king. The rest: frontal masks.

Temple of Jaguars (New): Toltec warriors in relief. This is behind the ball court.

El Castillo. This is the newest and largest of the pryamids. It has nine terraces, 4 stairways, 91 steps each, flanked by ramps in the form of a serpent. There is one step on top before the temple or sanctuary entrance, thus a total of 365 for the 365 days of the solar year.

The temple on top has 4 doors flanked by columns with serpents.

The ball court. (New part).
It is the largest of all Meso-America. 166 X 68 meters. It has vertical walls, at the bottom with low relief carvings of two teams watching the beheading of the captain of the losing team. This is Post-Classic, Mexican influence.

The Caracol (Observatory).
The old part. It is round and sets on top of two rectangular, angular platforms. The Caracol is newer, built later than the platforms. The round construction is late Classic, of the style also seen in Uxmal, that is, the Puuc. It may be that the round construction is imported from Central Mexico and is associated with the Cult of Quetzalcóatl (the Q. temple in Aztec Tenochtitlán would also be round, but built at least two centuries later than the Caracol, so we may have a contradiction here). Q. is associated with round temples in his form as Wind god. The top: small, rectangular windows used possibly for astronomical observation.

Human Sacrifice in the Cenote (New Chichén).

"If the victims survived past noon, they were fished out and asked for predictions of the coming year." It is connected to the main site of "new" Chichén by a "sacbé" or road of stones, the road some 300 meters long. They have found 50 skulls, some objects of copper and gold, masks and the famous gold disks depicting human sacrifice or losing warriors.

The "Tzomplantli" or Skull Stone.

It has many vertical rows of skulls on posts. This is a Post-Classic Mexican phenomenon, later adopted by the Aztecs in Tenochtitlán.

Other Mexican traits in Chichén: the chacmool (horizontal warrior, perhaps rain god) from Tula, the "tzompantli", the feathered serpents.

Temple of the Warriors (new Chichén).

The temple on top is held up by columns with feathered serpents. At the bottom of the stairs are 1000 columns, most with sculpted warriors inspired by Building B at Tula (Ttoltec culture, central Mexico). The columns are thought to be the remains of ruins; they held up a roof and below were "meeting rooms."

At the top of the stairway, before the entrance to the temple is a large "chacmool," a reclining warrior with an "offering plate" on its stomach. The Chacmool is from Central Mexico, Tula, and later Tenochtitlán. A possible rain god.

At the back of the Temple of the Warriors there is a plumed serpent, here "representing Venus or the Morning Star."

Murals at Chichén.

There are murals in the interior wallls of the Temple of the Jaguars and the interior of the Temple of the Warriors, the latter discovered by Stephens and Catherwood. The latter depict scenes of warriors at the edge of the sea. Those in the Temple of the Jaguars depict a battle directed by two chiefs, one with a sun emblem, another with plumed serpent.

Not mentioned but important: the interior temple within the large pyramid or the "Castillo." There is a large Chacmool but also a jaguar with an "offering plate" with jade eyes etc.

XIV. THE MAYA WORLD TODAY, SAN CRISTOBAL DE LAS CASAS IN CHIAPAS

The town sits at 2120 meters high or 6000 ft. and was planned out by Bernal Díaz del Castillo in 1524 during the battle of Chamula. It became a reality in 1528 when the Conquistador Diego de Mazariegos defeated the local tribes, but only lived a few months in the area. The city has always lived between fears of Indian uprisings (1712, 1869) and alliances with them. Indians represent 35 per cent of the population.

There is a mountain climate. The local pine, the "ocote", gave the name to places like Ocosingo on the way to Palenque. Wood is used for furniture and needles from the pine trees are spread on the floor of churches on feast days, an example being San Juan Chamula church.

This part of Chiapas is also an area of rebellion, dissension, and desires for self-autonomy. Local natives fought against the 1910 Revolution and this is the site of the 1994 Zapatista Rebellion.

The "zocalo" of San Cristóbal features the Cathedral constructed in the 16th century, the façade finished in 1696.

The "Iglesia de San Nicolás,'" was built and designated originally for black slaves after disease had decimated the Indians.

El Convento de Santo Domingo dates from 1546 and sports a façade of the "águila bicéfala" or royal arms of the Spanish Hapsburgs. The "Iglesia de Santo Domingo" to the side was finished by end of 17th (similar to La Merced in Antigua, Guatemala).

A Highlight of San Cristóbal de las Casas is its Indian Market

In 1711-12 there was a rebellion by all the Indians in the region against the repression of Spanish landholders and the church.

An important local event is Carnival in San Juan Chamula, held the last five days of the year, the days of transition in the Maya calendar.

LaterTimes: Guatemala, Antigua, the highlands with Lake Atitlán and . . .

Chichicastenango—The Mayas Today

There are three million Mayan speakers with nine language families.

ex. 400 Lacandones

ex. 800,000 Yucatecan Mayas
ex. One million Quiché-Cakchiquel-Tzutuhil speakers in highlands of Guatemala

Their cosmic tree is the "ceiba" or "miraguano": the navel of the earth, and of heaven

1. Mayan Towns

They were set up at the end of the conquest, with the following city plan:

The plaza and cosmic tree
Votive chapel (in each "barrio") with a patron saint
"Lavadero," or community wash basin
Altar dedicated to ancestors
Fountain
Church
Presbytery (house of priest)
Mayoralty (civil building)

2. Maya lands and Concepts Related to Them

The "ejido" is a square league of land, communal land.
Mayan concept: the earth is a square surrounded by four seas and set according to the sun.
The mountains: ancient pyramids
Church with steps: steps to heaven
Caves: tombs, access to the "infraworld"

3. The Municipality.

It is under the direction of a mayor, not elected but named. Work is collective work for the purpose of repairing roads or building bridges in the municipality. This concept and practice was abused by landholders and the government for their own projects (it harkens back to "repartimiento" days).

Mayor's insignia of power: a wooden shaft with steel tip

The Municipal Council.

It is responsible for maintenance, police and fiscal matters. It meets on festival days or market days under the "corredor" or varanda of the "ayuntamiento" or mayoral building. Then they meet with the public, hear complaints, petitions and judge quarrels.

There is a division of power between the church (priest, brotherhoods) and society (the municipality).

Healers, shamen, or "curanderos" are seen in the local religion and exist to predict the future and to cure sickness.

How do you know if a given person is or could be a shaman? He gets his powers by dreams or as an apprentice for years to other priests. But the priest is sometimes also seen as a "brujo" or witch, capable of changing himself into an animal.

The shamen also keep track of the days of the calendar; they are the modern "day counters" for both calendars, the ritual of 260 days, the solar of 365.

The shaman must know the words or language of the "curandero"—which words to use to heal, to predict and must know the way to get in touch with supernatural forces or powers and use them to heal sickness.

To see the future they consult clear stones, quartz crystals or seeds kept in a "bolsa." They use these to count time, and to make prophecies based on the 260 day calendar. Each day has a number and symbol.

Profecy sessions. The shaman answers questions of the public by observing the crystals and seeds thrown on a napkin or cloth placed on a table or the ground. Each rock, crystal or seed corresponds to a day of the calendar and a combination of number and sign. The reading or connotation marks good or bad, success or failure. Example: success of a wedding, a planting date, date to start a house.

Shaman healing: it is largely empirical knowledge: of fractures, extracting venom, herbs for medicine. The idea is to put the individual back in unity with the cosmos, society.

Shaman knowledge of beliefs: how to retrieve a lost soul, circulation of vital fluids in the body, how to identify and heal or get rid of evil agents introduced into the body by another "brujo" or shaman. Can call on supernatural powers, how how to use ritual discourse.

4. The religious brotherhoods "cofradías" and local fiestas or feast days.

The Spaniards imposed the cult of saints and established the brotherhoods to be responsible for the saint in the town.

The "cofradía" received in exchange land and cattle, and it helped cover the tribute charged each year by the crown to the community.

19th Century. During the political period of Liberalism, many Catholic missionaries and their orders were expulsed, so the brotherhoods actually grew in power. Syncretism, or the mixture of religious beliefs between native and Catholic, grew and was evidenced in a mixed liturgy.

ex. The church of Chichicastenago in Guatemala; the church of San Juan Chamula in Chiapas
ex. The church of Santiago Atitlán with its brotherhood "Cofradía de la Santa Cruz" and its saint, "Maximón," made of wood, the lord of luck, protector of "brujos."

Each saint has a votive "cofradía" and chapel where the saint is kept and an altar.

Recall the curious custom in towns where the saint is taken out "de paseo" with music and later returned to the chapel, a sort of procession to get him/her out and about. (The author experienced this frequently in his travels in Guatemala.) The explanation is that each saint has a feast day with a procession. They wake it, animate it and carry it (perhaps like the old Maya concept of the personage with the spirit on its back).

Use of incense in the modern Maya rituals in the chapels, local churches.

You can see the smoke rising from "petardos" or crude incense burners which they swing on the steps outside the church. The smoke is "the souls of the ancestors and the living are joined in one sweet smelling cloud." There are fireworks: rockets, bombs and firecrackers set off: to mark the different phases of the rituals.

5.   Liturgical feasts.

The Marian Cult and Events of Life of Christ exist for clergy and "ladinos." In Guatemala, "ladino" is white, European; in other areas, "ladino" may be Mestizo.
The Christmas cycle: Christimas, Epiphany
Easter (carnival, Holy Week, Ascension of Lord, Pentecost, Corpus Cristi)
All saints day
All souls day
Holy Week: each day is an episode in the Passion of Christ.
All Souls: night of November 1, all to the cemetery with food and drink for dead souls
Carnival: the origin is not sure but there are two meanings: European Carnival and Local Mythology
The most famous Carnival is in Chiapas, Church of San Juan Batista in Chamula.
Christmas itself is almost not celebrated in the Indian towns; it is more an urban festival with "Posadas."

Indian local festivals. The dances and use of masks were Pre-Columbian, but the Spanish adapted them to their advantage.

1 "Cristianos y Moros." Christians and Moors. Victory of Christians in the Iberian Peninsula over the Arabs.
2 "Baile de Cortés." This is a dance commemorating the victory of Cortés on horseback defeating Moctezuma. St. George and the Dragon. (good/evil).
3 The "Patzka". Dancers in rags are armed with canes, depicting animals, and wearing masks of the "bearded ones." "Personifies the ancestors of the people of Rabinal (Guatemala) who used to take their saint to the main altar of the Catholic Church, causing the sun to rotate and rain to fall."
4 Los Voladores. "The Flyers." It originated in Central Mexico and pre-conquest times in Guatemala. Two groups of actors, the "monos" and the "ángeles" climb pole, tie ropes to ankles, rotate gradually to earth. (See our illustrations from Yucatán near Tulum.)
5 The "Rabinal Achí." This Pre-Hispanic dance is old Quiché, about the trial of an accused Quiché warrior, his judgment and sacrifice.
6 Music and musical instruments in the festivals.

Flutes, drums, violín, harp, guitar. The instruments are often homemade, rustic and "out of tune."

The marimba comes from the xyolphone, and was introduced in the 16th century. It is of African origin from slaves and is now the national instrument of Guatemala Indians.

6. Indian Markets.

One sees artisan products, photographs for souvenirs, shoe shiners, charlatans and predictions of the future. ex. Antigua, Chichicastenango (Curran saw the same with the Indios Guambianos, in Silvia, Colombia) The Indians are quiet, bargain in low voices, and are not aggressive in behavior with arguing or advertising.

7. Domestic economy

The first activity is agriculture, but much of it is done by women because men are on work contracts on the coast on large plantations. They cultivate corn and chile. The "milpa" or the "huerta." Artisan activity supplements the income but is not principal source.

Examples: articles of clay, ceramics, dolls, wooden horses, "losa" or china plates from clay and painted, palm leaves for hats and mats, and most important, textiles. Also some masks, made of wood, carved and painted, maybe of leather, for dances and tourists.

8. Maya Weaving.

The weavings may depict history, myth and legend. The best are seen in Chiapas, Mexico, and the Guatemalan highlands. The use of wool was introduced by the Spanish by virtue of sheep and goats. Today acrylics are used in many cases.

el huipil (blouse)
la falda (skirt)
la cinta (ribbon for hair)
el tzute (covering for head in the "cofradía")
el rebozo (shawl)

"Mundo Maya" has examples from different pueblos.

Men in pre-hispanic times used:

la capa
el taparrabos
la túnica
el cinturón
las sandalias
(Headdress of quetzal feathers were in use for nobles; jade jewels)

Now:

Camisola (over blouse)
Camisa de cuello briscado (collared shirt)
Pantalón (hand women trousers)
Tzute: head covering

Symbolism of dress and patterns in weaving

The composition or design in a "huipil" can be read as a text.

a. Diamonds ("rombo") 3 levels: heaven, earth and infraworld. Jesus Christ in middle.
b. Vultures and bees. Placed below rows of diamonds. Vulture: has to do with local mythology Bees: has to do with family of the weaver
c. The "germination" on the sleeve of the "huipil." This has to do with the cycle of plant germination, may have symbols from Maya calendar, to invoke the benevolence of the gods.

d. Anthropomorphic symbols symbolize the forces of nature of local mythologies. ex. wild animals

ex. The two headed eagle (on Curran's "tzute") may have link to Spanish Hapsburg symbol, may have other.

** The link of the weavings to the stelae. Ex. Dintel n. 24 of Yaxchilán, 719 AD. Queen Xoe has a huipil decorated with diamonds.

9.   Post Conquest Literature.

"The Book of the Popol Vuh." "The Book of Counsel" It was discovered in Chichicastenango by a Catholic Dominican Priest in 1701.

It is written in Latin Characters or alphabet but in Maya Quiché language and was written down in the first years after the Conquest. It is a body of knowledge and beliefs:

The "Popol Vuh" tells of the Genesis of the Universe

Battle of forces of life and death
Creation of "men of corn" (first man was of ice, then wood, and finally of corn)
Ancestral gestation of different tribes
Geneological memory of the sovereigns of Utatlán

Post-Conquest Literature. the play "The Rabinal Achí."

So end the professor's notes to "Mundo Maya."

5. NOTES FROM MAJOR DOCUMENTARY FILMS ON THE MAYA

SCENES FROM THE VIDEO "CENTRAL AMERICA: THE BURDEN OF TIME"

Even though the following notes are cryptic, most often one-liners, they do give an indication first of all of what the film covered, but even without seeing the films (and all can be searched on "Google"), often times the one-liners will add to our appreciation of the topics of this book. As mentioned, these films were shown regularly in SPA 472, Spanish American Civilization, at ASU when we were studying Pre-Coloumbian civilizations.

I. Los Mayas en Guatemala

Tikal
The spiritual conquest of the Indians never took place.
Chichicastenango: shamen doing Cakchiquel rites
La Iglesia de Santo Tomás, Chichicastengango, shamen burning copal
Mercado de Chichicastenango
A native jacket with the Bat Symbol (the bat was also seen on stelae at Tikal) from the town of Sololá
The religious brotherhood in Chichicastenango is organizing the feast day
Inside scene from the church of Santo Tomás in Chichicastenango showing the "cofradía" and Maya rituals
The "Popol Vuh" was copied down here in this town.
Totonicapán (Guatemala) rituals
Utatlán: the last Maya-Quiché capital. The conquistador Alvarado destroyed it.
Rituals done there as described in the <u>Popol Vuh</u>
Fiesta o festival en Momostenango
Shamán
Scene of the Lake of Atitlán

II. Cultures in Mexico

Las Ventas—the Olmec heads
The art of the Olmecs goes back almost 3000 years.
Famous art figure from the Olmecas
Valle de México: View from on top of the pyramids at Teotihuacan
Teotihuacán: "the place where men became gods"
Pirámide del Sol
Rooms excavated below the Pyramid of the Sun
Teotihuacán: the first true urban civilization in Mesoamerica.

III. Then, chronologically: Copán

5th-9th century A.D. The dynasties
The first king was called 18 Rabbitt, a stela from October, 721 A.D.
July of 736 A.D. 18 Rabbitt was taken prisoner by a rival king and was beheaded.
Writing was invented here independently of the old world.
The hieroglyphic stairway contains the longest single inscription in pre-colombian civilization
The last king was Yax Pak in 820 A.D.
Last inscription in Copán: 822 A.D.
Tikal was deserted around the same time.
So the classic Mayan cities were gone: their collapse is still a mystery in spite of many theories.
The narrator conjectures: was the land exhausted? Perhaps the civilization "lost its nerve."
A painting from Tikal, "the place where the count of days was kept."

IV. Back to Mexico City

Mexico City
The "Mexica" or Azteca, 14th century (1325)
Tenochtitlán their capital
The Aztecs in the 15th Century
Aztec Masks
The statue of Coatlicue discovered in 1790, now in the "Museo Nacional"
La Plaza Mayor-el Templo mayor
Temple of the skulls

The narrator notes: there is a basic contradiction in regard to the Aztecs: the aesthetically high quality of their art in juxtaposition to the thousands of sacrificial victims in order to continue life.

Aztec solidarity with the universe
A painting of Tenochtitlán by Diego Rivera
The main plaza of old Mexico City: El Zócalo de México
The arrival of Hernán Cortés corresponded to the predicted return of Quetzalcóatl.
The fatalistic defeat of the Aztecs by the Spaniards

V. The Age of the Spanish Conquest

Antigua, Guatemala
Volcán del Água
Capuchinas

Spanish genocide in the Americas
80-90 per cent of Indian population died, up to 50 million
Padre José de Acosta
Marimba mass in Guatemala
Fray Bartolomé de las Casas and his defense of the Indians
Bartolomé was later named Bishop in Cobán in Guatemala
Services in the Catholic church of Cobán in Maya-Quiché language
Las Casas came to realize that his views on the Indians fit the black slaves as well, but the realization came too late.
1550. The famous debate in Valladolid in Espana: Las Casas versus Sepúlveda. Are Indians not rational beings with a mortal soul?
Las Casas won the moral battle, but slavery came anyway.

The last Maya Stronghold (during the conquest)

It was located in the Petén at Flores in Guatemala
The Indian stronghold fell 150 years after the original Spanish conquest by Alvarado
The coincidence: it fell 13 katuns later (1697); 13 katuns before was the first conquest
A catastrophe: this was the Mayan Burden of Time.

In 1954, 260 years later (13 katuns) after the fall of Flores, a U.S. led coup took place which was considered a modern disaster for Guatemalan Indians.

VI. Modern Guatemala:

There was guerilla warfare in the 1980s. There were some 40,000 dead and perhaps one million persons displaced.
A Zunil procession: taking the "santos" or guardians of the community on an outing "de paseo."
Indians submerged today in the city (Av. 6a. Guatemala)
View of Atitlán
Festival of "8 Monkey." This is a modern Cakchiquel festival of the "Day Keepers."
Their means of identity is kept by "keeping the time."
The final scene: Tikal

NOTES FROM THE VIDEO "LOST KINGDOM OF THE MAYAS" JANUARY, 1993

Scenes:

The Mayas. Copán.
1839. The Stephens and Catherwood trip, drawings.
The Southern Lowlands
The "gok" pile: "God only knows" (the original stones are scattered and strewn about).
Tikal: the New York of the Mayas (size, importance)
Copán: the Paris of the Mayas (culture)
The Mayas had no interest in metal, thus no gold was to be found.

1993. One-half of the glyphs have been deciphered. David Stuart, epigrapher.
Mayan codices were burned in Yucatán, but four major remain.
They were close to our concept of the almanaque: information.

The Mayas traced the movement of the stars and constellations in the skies over thousands of years, in the past and into the future. They could predict eclipses.

Their universe or cosmology was based on the idea of cyclical time, cycles that repeat themselves. Time had its own life.

We know much of this because of the glyphs on the codices and on the stelae.

The hieroglyphic stairway in Copán: the greatest stone document of the New World, 1200 stones with glyphs. Epigrapher Linda Schele a major decipherer, U. of Texas.

Her thesis: the idea of historical consciousness and the goal of "writing it down" as a major step in any civilization. American history really begins in 250 BC when the Mayas began their glyphs.

The beginning was an agricultural society.
AD 400 marked the first buildings of stone in Copán
Articles which were found there: cacau, quetzal feathers, jade.

The ball game: players had belts with heads hung from them. Metaphoric meaning of the game: the movement of the ball imitated the movement of the cosmos, the sun and stars. If the game were played "right," all would go okay in the cosmos.

The gods were the source of all life, and only kings had the power to communicate with them. The gods sustain the universe and humans must sustain the gods. Acts of sacrifice open the doorway to communicate with the gods. An example is the burning of paper strips with the drippings of blood from genital bloodletting of the king himself. Keep in mind: the Maya were <u>not</u> a western society so we cannot understand them in western terms.

The Maya today:
Guatemala (the Cakchiqueles) Priests.
Burning of copal (incense) in the church of Chichicastenango today. The Cakchiquel brotherhoods or "cofradías" in Chichicastenango demonstrate a blend of Catholicism and Maya religion.

In Chiapas, Mexico. Scenes of Mayan ladies with their blouses or "huipiles:" the head emerges in the center of the "huipil" which signifies the center of the world, just as the great tree of life emerges from the earth. Interviews with weavers: "It came to my heart in a dream." How they learned to weave and the patterns they weave.

One scholar says the modern patterns of the "huipiles" can be seen on some of the stelae. They are designs of a "map of the world," not the geographic world, but images of a sacred universe, a dream world, a sacred universe of the gods.

Remember: everything is more than it seems in the Maya world.

The Mayan place of fright: where you go when you die, the underworld, dark, inhabited by snakes, etc.

Caracol: a prosperous administrative Mayan center with many tombs. It fought and defeated no less than Tikal.

A Mayan custom: bury the dead under the floor of the house. If nobility, under the floors of temples.

Note: There is a similarity to central Mexico and the Aztecs as seen in Carlos Fuentes' "<u>La región más transparente del aire</u>" ("Where the Air is Clear").

The Mayan tomb is like a time capsule: it gives us dates and names of personages from the materials in it, i.e. the glyphs on the ceramics.

Maya buildings are built one on top of another at certain time spans, most often with changes in generations of a dynasty. When a new ruler was ready to be buried, they collapsed the top of the building immediately below his (they were built at each Katún, 20 years).

NB. Note the tunnel and tomb at Palenque

Copán, temple 16. They have found huge well-preserved masks in the interior of temple, perfectly preserved. Question: why did the Mayas not deface or destroy these when they built on top as was normally the case? This temple is called "Rosalilla" by the archeologists. They also found blackened flint stone carved objects; flint was the fire stone, with ceremonial figures with faces, perhaps ancestors or victims. Found 9 flints, perhaps to correspond with the 9 Maya lords of the night.

7th century A.D. Copán was at its peak. There were cities, "roads", (sacbés), and evidence of trade.

562 A.D. Caracol attacks and defeats Tikal. Members of Tikal's royal family leave, migrate and establish Dos Pilas.

Scholar Demarest (Vanderbilt). The digs at Dos Pilas prove the Mayas were a very warlike people with constant warfare, at first ritualized, later on a much larger scale, a sort of "arms race." Original war may have consisted in battles between dynasties, for succession.

1990: Demarest and colleagues discovered the fortified wall at Dos Pilas built on top of the old hieroglyphic stairs. The new wall was made with stones torn from the major buildings in the main plazas—to defend the city and fortify it.

8th century: Ritualized warfare grew into what seem to be campaigns of expansion on the Río de la Pasión. It was a war for conquest, an "arms race." (Demarest)

8th-9th century: 700-800 A.D. At Caracol there are signs of increased warfare, sacrifices increased, people now may die instead of becoming slaves. It marked the end of that period.

Eventually: the power of the kings was destroyed and people retreated into the forest, back to agricultural existence. (Demarest's theory)

End of the film.

NOTES FROM THE VIDEO "THE BLOOD OF KINGS" a Time-Life Video

Introduction

There is a sacred world where a game is being played, but a game played for their lives! 750 A.D. But mysteries remain today to understand this civilization. Europe was in the Dark Ages when this civilization was flourishing with its arts and sciences in Central America.

Its greatest city was Tikal in the Petén of lowlands Guatemala, a city of 40,000 people, the size of Manhattan Island. One hundred years later it was abandoned. It is an example of the fragility of all civilization according to Professor Demarest of Vanderbilt, excavator at Caracol and adviser for this film.

But Tikal was not destroyed; it was abandoned. The people "just walked away." Why?
Perhaps because of the deepest beliefs of its people and the changes in them. It is a mystery, but they did leave clues.

One clue is the Maya hieroglyphic writing, a code written on "paper," stone and ceramics.

Origins of the Maya: their ancestors were among the Asiatic peoples who crossed the Behring Sea during the Ice Age. The primeval Maya came thousands of years later from 40,000 to 25,000 B.C.

The Classic Maya were from 250 to 900 A.D. The civilization lasted six centuries, and then it was over, "they walked away." The ruins were "lost" for one thousand years; the modern discovery was by John Stephens and William Catherwood in 1839. Their prose account and illustrations is called "Incidents of Travel in Central America, Chiapas and the Yucatan and it captured the romance and mystery of the Mayas plus gave clues as to their essence. Early explorers suspected that it was an ORIGINAL civilization, developed in Central America and not from elsewhere. A unique culture. The key, surmised Stephens, was in the glyphs.

Stephens and Catherwood opened a new era of exploration. Adventurers and eccentrics then came, looking not only for buried treasure, but for answers to the riddle of a lost civilization whose understanding was elusive. There were monuments, hundreds of pyramids and stelae, but no answers. Their purpose? A mystery.

It all changed in 1957 (the date 1952 may apply). Mexican archeologist Alberto Rus excavating at Palenque discovered the stairway to the Temple of the Inscriptions which led to Pacal's tomb. Scenes of the crypt, the stairway, the crowning temple. But Rus did not know who the cadaver was and why he merited so much ceremony at his death. Who was the man behind the mask?

The main clue once again was the writing system—the glyphs. They were cryptic, coded and opaque. They had to be deciphered. Why were the cities abandoned?

The next development. The codices or Mayan "books" proved to be an independently invented writing system, one of five in the entire world. They were "texts imbued with magic." They contained a description of the Mayan cosmos (universe) and chronicles of their dreams and were as momentous as the hieroglyphics of ancient Egypt; they were the first written language of the New World.

The story of Bishop Landa of the 16th century conquest times in the Yucatan. He had the Spanish alphabet (24 letters) "translated" to the Mayan glyphs that corresponded to their sounds (but there are 800 glyphs known)! Yet when he discovered that Mayas supposedly converted to Catholocism were still actually practicing the old religion, he became irate (according to art historian Mary Ellen Miller in the film) and ordered all the codices to be burned. A total of thousands of texts were burned (one might check this total) in the entire conquest. So it was ironic—the man most dedicated to saving the Mayan souls and their culture helped destroy it. The film calls the texts "a literary record of Mayan lives." Only four texts escaped and they were sent to Europe by Cortés and others.

The first glyphs to be deciphered had to do with numbers and the mathematical system. Math was tied to astronomy; the Mayas did a detailed observation of the night sky and calculated and recorded it in detail.

The next scholar was Eric Thompson in the 1950s. He concluded that the Mayas were a people dedicated to the study of the heavens and the meaning of time. He thought they were ruled by "priests-astronomers."

The Mayas did succeed in calculating and recording celestial events one half billion years in the past and recorded all this 1000 years ago. Thompson thought they were a theocratic, peaceful people who worshiped time and were ruled by priest-astronomers who worked in sacred observatories. Thompson thus had an idealized notion and a thawed theory. (The film is a little too hard on him Curran thinks.)

An example of Maya astronomy and math is the "Castillo" at Chichén-Itzá (note that is a Toltec and not purely Maya building). It has 365 steps and is aligned precisely with the sun's movements to show spring and fall equinoxes (the undulating serpent).

The codices mapped the position of the stars and planets for years to come and even predicted solar eclipses. It must have seemed to the commoners that their leaders "controlled the heavens."

The Maya Calendars. One is the solar of 365 days; the other the 260 day ritual calendar. The two meshed like gears, a given day only repeating itself each 52 years. The May calendar showed the astrological significance of each day. It was accurate: the calculation of the cycles of the moon done 1500 years ago is off only 33 seconds today.

The Mayas placed a specific date for the creation of the world, 3014 B.C. and a specific date for the end of time, December 23, 2012.

A scene of the day-counters in today's Guatemala.

But the glyphs told more: Justin Kerr, a photographer by trade, used camera and ceramic vases to make a scrolled text. His work revealed a people obsessed with the fearful and the bloody gods of the underworld or the infraworld. The underworld was a hellish place, ex. The god of decapitation. An ominous place.

Other Ominous Customs.

The deformation of children's skulls with wooden boards
Maya women's teeth were drilled with holes into which jade or turquoise beads were inserted as
   signs of beauty.
Mind altering drugs were used; one fresco shows a Mayan smoking what appears to be a big
   "reefer."
Intoxicants were smoked, but alcohol seems to be the drug of choice. Mary Ellen Miller believes
   they drank to excess with the purpose of vomiting, thus using the alcohol as a sort of
   "enema." But why? She does not say, but one supposes to "cleanse the system."

The next breakthrough involved the photographer and film maker Giles Healy when he was shown the frescos of Bonampak by a Lacandon Indian in 1946. They exposed a savage truth: warfare for captives, human torture, sacrifice, and bloodletting for bloodthirsty deities. The utopian vision is gone. Miller says the scenes depict the tearing off of captives' fingernails, blood dripping, decapitation, etc.

Eric Thompson went to Bonampak but refused to accept the ideas of bloodshed, torture, etc. He called the scene a "nasty raid" and thought the captives had dipped their hands in paint, "or something like that" according to Miller.

The next breakthrough takes place in May, 1945, when the Russians arrive in Berlin and the national library was burning. A Russian officer picks up a book at random and it turns out to be "Reproduction of Surviving Mayan Codices." He takes it home, becomes interested and delves into its text. He then passes the book on to Tatiana Proskoriakov. She makes great strides in deciphering Mayan writing, coming to know the glyphs for birth and death. Experts could now "read" glyphs and saw stones, stelae, etc. as funerary monuments and learned of real Maya history. They came to know the names of Maya royalty, ex. 18 Rabbit at Copán. The Mayans' ancestors and conquests were all revealed on the stones! 18 Rabbit was tenth in line at Copán and ruled for almost 70 years!

Scholars came to find that the stelae depicted monarchs or kings who ruled and commanded cities with an absolute power, disdain of others and arrogance. The big question became: what was the source of the Maya kings' authority? Was it power? Riches? Why did people submit to such tyrannical authority? What was the underlying source of power? "It was based on belief." (Demarest, Vanderbilt)

The Maya king's powers were connected to self-immolation, bloodletting. Using a "knife" made of a sting ray's stinger or a rope with thorns, the king and his wife shed their own blood. The blood was considered to be sacred.

Every portal of every Maya temple is a doorway to the underworld (i.e. the doorway is the Earth Monster's jaws). Inside that temple it is the duty of both the king and the queen to reenact the mythical moment of Mayan creation: in myth it was the blood of the gods which gave life to man, the original act of sacrifice. On earth the king is as a god so blood is the price of power, the debt to the gods which must be repaid. Myth and symbols do not suffice; blood must be shed and royal blood at that, from the tongue or genitals of the king and queen. Such bloodletting binds the sacrifice of the gods to the lives of men.

Once sacrificed, the blood rises up to the gods (blood was dripped on paper and burned, the smoke went up as a prayer and sacrifice). The gods acknowledge the sacrifice causing the sun to rise, the corn to grow, rain, good crops, success in battle, etc. (The rising smoke from the burning of incense or copal in Maya communities today serves, probably, the same purpose, that is, of prayers or communications with the gods.)

Linda Schele, perhaps the best of recent Mayanists said that in the New World people believed that the soul, the part of you passed on to your children and grandchildren, the eternal thing about you, resides in your blood. So if you wish to give the greatest offering, you give your blood. Blood is the most powerful substance on earth; the king's blood is more potent than that of others because of his history—his heritage, his antecedents.

But all the Mayas gave blood at one time or another, a self-giving and self-sacrifice. Other means existed as well: the blood of captives, the blood of losers in the ball game. The Maya reveled in this terror. There are ceramics which show the pain of the sacrificial victim; the Bonampak frescos show it as well.

Yet today Maya shamen practice blood sacrifice, but with chickens. The ancestral beliefs are intact, but in another context.

Christianity may have been forced on the Maya, but it struck a note with them: the concept of a god who sacrificed his own deity (blood) for man is not at all unfamiliar to them. They could accept Jesus Christ's sacrifice because their own kings did the same thing in antiquity. The Christian concept of a divine being shedding his own blood for mankind made perfect sense.

For the ancient Mayas the king's blood was the mortar that bound all life together. The king's sacrifice of his own blood assured the stability of man in the world and the sanction of the gods in the peoples' beliefs. The king stood at the center of the universe; remove the king and the system comes crashing down.

When the Mayas lost faith in their king or kings, problems began. Authority was based on belief. Failure undermines the whole system and cannot be adjusted for. So soil erosion, defeats in war, and overpopulation came, and the king was held responsible. If all seemed to fail, it was a sign that he failed them (and blood sacrifice was insufficient). So sacrifice was increased. In a related way, this was the reason for the excess of Aztec sacrifice in 1487 with the new "Templo Mayor" plus the belief they were living in the final phase of the universe and had to avoid destruction at all cost!

The amazing thing is not the end of the Mayas, but the fact that this system could have lasted so long, 700 years, and an oppressive civilization (Demarest).

The Mayas were self-made, self-contained, unique and wholly original. The great dynasties were built on the faith of the people, and when the crops failed and enemies won battles, the people lost the faith, the rulers lost power and as the power diminished, the people abandoned their cities, and the jungle reclaimed the stones (Demarest).

End of the Film

Mark Curran

Curran's comments.

These theories are very current now in 2002; Demarest, Miller, and Linda Schele (deceased) are recognized leaders in current theory.

A query: evidence seems to be with the film and its advisors, and certainly with the deciphering of some say 80 per cent of the glyphs. The scholars in this film are probably more correct than anyone prior to them. But it is possible, even likely, that future research may add to their theories, perhaps disprove some of part of them, or perhaps not. Still, I sympathize with Thompson from the 1950s and with him wishing it all could have remained a simpler, less violent, gentler and more intellectual Maya world. My earliest interest took place with trips to sites in 1976, sites which have been modified by new discoveries since then (Demarest's at Caracol and Dos Pilas, Honduran Fursia at Copán, Schele's work at Copán). The blood and violence theories are the latest.

One question: conquering armies and civilizations have always imprisoned, tortured and even killed the losers, but not necessarily shedding their blood as a sacred sacrifice. Simple vengeance, power and other motives can also exist as well. But in Mesoamerica the "Guerra florida" or "Flower War" for captives for sacrifice was central to the Aztec worldview. And the warrior-sacrifice worldview found in Chichén-Itzá was found first at Teotihuacán and Tula with the Toltecs who migrated to the Yucatan. Whatever the worldview, it was general to the entire area.

It is quite clear that the shedding of blood, even "sacred blood," to maintain the course of the universe and gain favor with the gods, or even to offer blood as food to the gods, was a primary and central belief in most of Mesoamerica at that time, i.e. the "Toltec" and then the Aztec traditions.

Food for thought.

ABOUT THE AUTHOR

Mark Curran is a retired professor from Arizona State University where he worked from 1968 to 2011. He taught Spanish and Brazilian Portuguese languages and their respective cultures. He researched Brazil's folk-popular literature, "A Literatura de Cordel," and has published many scholarly articles and ten books in Brazil, Spain and the United States on the subject. "The Farm," published in 2010 was a change of pace to the auto-biographical, recollections of growing up on a family farm in central Kansas in the 1940s and 1950s. "Coming of Age with the Jesuits" chronicles seven years in Jesuit College and graduate school and his first forays to Latin America. "Adventures of a 'Gringo' Researcher in Brazil in the 1960s" tells of one year of dissertation research in that country. "A Trip to Colombia—Highlights of Its Spanish Colonial Heritage" tells of travel and research in that country in 1975 in preparation for his specialty in Spanish at ASU. Now, "Travel, Research and Teaching in Guatemala and Mexico" tells of times in those countries with the research emphasis on their Pre-Columbian Civilizations.

Books Published:

A Literatura de Cordel, Brazil, 1973
Jorge Amado e a Literatura de Cordel, Brazil, 1981
A Presença de Rodolfo Coelho Cavalcante e a Moderna Literatura de Cordel, Brazil, 1987
La Literatura de Cordel-Antología Bilingüe-Español y Portugués, Spain, 1990
Cuíca de Santo Amaro-Poeta Repórter da Bahia, Brazil, 1991
História do Brasil em Cordel, Brazil, 1998
Cuíca de Santo Amaro-Controvérsia em Cordel, Brazil, 2000
Brazil's Folk-Popular Poetry—"A Literatura de Cordel" A Bilingual Anthology in English and Portuguese, USA, 2010
The Farm, Growing Up in Abilene, Kansas, in the 1940s and 1950s, USA, 2010
Retrato do Brasil em Cordel, Brazil, 2011
Coming of Age with the Jesuits, USA, 2012
Adventures of a 'Gringo' Researcher in Brazi in the 1960s, USA, 2012
Peripécias de um Pesquisador 'Gringo' no Brasil nos Anos 1960, USA, 2012
A Trip to Colombia-Highlights of Its Spanish Colonial Heritage, USA, 2013
Travel, Research and Teaching in Guatemala and Mexico. In Search of the Pre-Columbian Heritage. 2 volumes. USA, 2013

Mark Curran

Curran makes his home in Mesa, Arizona, and spends part of the year in Colorado. He is married to Keah Runshang Curran, and they have one daughter, Kathleen, who lives in Flagstaff, Arizona, and makes documentary films. Her film "Greening of the Revolution" was shown most recently at the Sonoma Film Festival in 2012.
Email: profmark@asu.edu
Webpage: www.currancordelconnection.com